LAW or
GRACE

LAW or GRACE

by

M. R. DE HAAN, M.D.

ZONDERVAN
PUBLISHING HOUSE
OF THE ZONDERVAN CORPORATION | GRAND RAPIDS, MICHIGAN 49506

LAW OR GRACE

Copyright 1965 by M. R. DeHaan, M.D.

Thirteenth printing 1981
ISBN 0-310-23401-8

Library of Congress Catalog Card No. 64-8842

Printed in the United States of America

Contents

INTRODUCTION

The first church council in the city of Jerusalem, as recorded in the fifteenth chapter of Acts, was necessitated by a question concerning the relationship of the believer to the law of Moses. Paul the Apostle had on his first missionary journey preached the Gospel of the grace of God, without the works of the law. Upon his return from his first missionary journey he had rehearsed to the church in Antioch "all that God had done with them, and how he had opened the door of faith unto the Gentiles" (Acts 14:27). Paul reported to the church how Gentiles had been saved, without becoming Jewish proselytes, or submitting to circumcision, or keeping the law of Moses. The Christians at Antioch rejoiced in the good news of the free grace of God.

These reports of Gentiles being saved by grace without the law, reached Jerusalem, where a group of legalistic Jews insisted that salvation necessitated placing these believers under the law. These legalists came to Antioch and began to teach the believers,

> . . . Except ye be circumcised after the manner of Moses, ye cannot be saved (Acts 15:1).

This started a real dispute between Paul and Barnabas on the one hand, and this group of "law preachers" on the other. A real row broke out. Dr. Luke reports it as follows:

> . . . Paul and Barnabas had no small dissension and disputation with them . . . (Acts 15:2).

Unable to settle the question, they decided to submit the problem to the apostles and elders at Jerusalem. A committee, including Paul and Barnabas, was appointed to go to the apostles in Jerusalem. Upon their arrival in the city they were welcomed by the church, to whom they reported all that the Gospel of God's grace had accomplished among the Gentiles. However, they were immediately opposed by the legalistic Pharisees who insisted,

> . . . That it was needful to circumcise them [the Gentiles], and to command them to keep the law of Moses (Acts 15:5).

Introduction

The apostles called the church together and tried to settle the controversy, but instead disorder broke out and the meeting resulted in a heated debate. There was much disputing between the two factions which we might well designate as the "grace party" and the "law party." Peter is the first to testify of his experience, and rehearses his visit to the Gentile household of Cornelius, saying that God "put no difference between us (Jews) and them (Gentiles), purifying their hearts by faith" (Acts 15:9). Peter calls the law of Moses a yoke which they themselves (the Jews) were unable to bear (Acts 15:10), and then concludes with his judgment of the matter:

> But we believe that through the grace of our Lord Jesus Christ we [Jews] shall be saved, even as they [Gentiles] (Acts 15:11).

Peter's speech came somewhat as a surprise to the legalists, the champions of the law; and without any more disputing, the assembly listened quietly to the testimony of Paul and Barnabas, corroborating the views of Peter. It was now time for James (apparently the chairman of the meeting) to speak. The silence which followed the testimonies of Peter, Paul and Barnabas, left the opposition speechless. However, it raised a serious question.

If the Lord was now building a Church, the Body of Christ, consisting of both Jews and Gentiles, while Jesus was in Heaven, then what about all the promises of the Scriptures concerning the Kingdom, and the reign of the Messiah on earth? All the prophets had clearly foretold that when Messiah should come, He would restore the Kingdom of Israel, deliver them from the Gentile yoke of bondage, and Israel as a nation would dwell in her repossessed land. Were all these prophecies to be cast aside? Must we spiritualize these promises and apply them now to the Church? If God is now calling out a Church, a body from among the Gentiles, is God then through with national Israel? These were questions which needed to be answered, and James rises to the occasion.

The explanation James gives is the essence of simplicity, yet scholars have been unable to grasp it. James says that all the promises to Israel concerning the Kingdom will be literally fulfilled, but *not at this time*. First, the Lord is going to carry out a part of His plan, which until now had been a mystery, and then after that, the Kingdom promises to Israel shall be realized. The words of James are clear:

> Simeon hath declared how God at the first did visit the Gentiles, to take out of them a people for his name (Acts 15:14).

This is what God was now doing. The Kingdom had been set aside, and God is now "calling out" from among the Gentiles a people for His Name—the Body of Christ—the Church. This, says James, was in full agreement with the prophecies concerning the Kingdom.

> . . . as it is written,
> *After this I* will return, and will build again the tabernacle of David, which is fallen down; and I will build again the ruins thereof, and I will set it up (Acts 15:15, 16).

After this I will return! After *what?* After He has gathered out from among the Gentiles a people for His Name. After this Body of the Church is complete, and the fullness of the Gentiles be come in, *then* the Lord will return and restore the nation of Israel, and will set up the Kingdom here on earth, and all the prophecies of Messiah's reign will be fulfilled to the letter.

Now comes the answer to the question which had brought them together. Are the believers of this Church age under the law of the Kingdom? Is the believer in this dispensation of grace subject to the laws laid down by Moses for the nation of Israel? James gives his sentence in the following words:

> Wherefore my sentence is, that we *trouble not* them, which from among the Gentiles are turned to God:
> But that we write unto them, that they abstain from pollutions of idols, and from fornication, and from things strangled, and from blood (Acts 15:19, 20).

Not a word about keeping the law of Moses, not a word about circumcision, but they were advised against three things: idolatry, fornication, and eating of blood. Abstinence from these things was advised, not on the basis of *law,* but grace. These Gentiles had been idolaters; fornication was in certain instances a religious rite; and they did not respect the sanctity of the blood. Because these three things, so common among the Gentiles and so abhorrent to the Jews, were to be especially guarded against, they are warned about them.

Introduction

A letter is addressed to the Gentiles at Antioch, and sent by the hand of Paul, Barnabas, and a company of others. The letter is in answer to the question, "Are the believers (especially of the Gentiles) under the law of Moses?" Here is a copy of the letter sent by the Jerusalem elders to Antioch:

> Forasmuch as we have heard, that certain which went out from us have *troubled* you with words, subverting your souls, saying, Ye *must be circumcised, and keep the law* . . . (Acts 15:24).

Notice again the problem. The legalists from Jerusalem had claimed that the Gentile Christians at Antioch must become Jews by submitting to circumcision, and *to keep the law*. Now notice the decision:

> . . . *to whom we gave no such commandment* (Acts 15:24b).

Those who teach that the Christians are under the law are *perverters* of the grace of God. "We never gave any such commandments," wrote the apostles and elders to the church at Antioch. The legalistic sabbatarians were unauthorized, and we now repudiate their demand for "we gave no such commandment." This was the message relayed to Antioch—"the Gentile believers are not under the law."

The letter was delivered to the church, "which when they had read, they rejoiced for the consolation" (Acts 15:31). The matter should have been settled, but the *law* teachers continued their practice of following Paul everywhere he went, trying to undo the *grace* preaching of Paul. Everywhere he traveled he was opposed. No less than three books of the New Testament were written to combat errors concerning the law. There were three errors present from the very beginning of the apostolic age. These were legalism, antinomianism, and Galatianism. Legalism teaches that men must be saved by keeping the law. This error is answered in Paul's epistle to the Romans. The second error was the exact opposite, teaching that it makes no difference how we live, for it is all of grace. This error is answered in the epistle of James. The third and most subtle of the errors is Galatianism. It is the teaching that we are saved by grace, and then we are to be kept by obeying the law perfectly; we are saved by faith alone, but then our ultimate salvation depends on our works.

Introduction

This error is called Galatianism because it was so prevalent in the Galatian churches, and Paul wrote one whole epistle to refute this error—the epistle to the Galatians.

These three errors are still with us today. Although the matter was settled in the first church council and expounded in the epistles, the errors have persisted. It is with the prayer and hope that these chapters may be used of the Lord to lead some precious souls out of the bondage and fear of the law into the liberty of God's grace, that this volume is sent forth, for

. . . where the Spirit of the Lord is, there is liberty (II Corinthians 3:17).

Chapter One

THE DEFINITION OF LAW

Is the believer under the law, under grace, or under both? This is a question which was settled almost two thousand years ago, and yet millions of Christians are completely confused, and fail to understand the clear distinction between the ministry of the law and the ministry of grace. The Bible, however, leaves no question about the matter. The law was never given to save anyone. Not one single sinner in all the history of the human race has ever been saved by keeping the law of God. In fact, God knew, before He ever gave Israel the law, and commanded them to obey it, that no one (except the Lord Jesus Himself) would ever keep that law of God perfectly; yea, more, He never expected anyone to keep it perfectly. We might multiply scriptures by the score to prove that the Bible teaches the absolute inability of the law to save a single sinner, or keep a single saint saved. We do not wish to weary you with a recitation of Scripture passages, but we must quote a few from among the many. In Romans 3:19 and 20, Paul says:

> Now we know that what things soever the law saith, it saith to them who are under the law: that every mouth may be stopped, and all the world may become guilty before God.
> Therefore by the deeds of the law there shall no flesh be justified in his sight: for by the law is the knowledge of sin, not salvation from sin (Romans 3:19, 20).

Or hear Paul once again in verse 28:

★ Therefore we conclude that a man is justified by faith without the deeds of the law (Romans 3:28).

Turning to Galatians we read:

> Knowing that a man is not justified by the works of the law, but by the faith of Jesus Christ, . . . for by the works of the law shall no flesh be justified (Galatians 2:16).

And in verse 21 Paul nails it down with finality and says:

> I do not frustrate the grace of God: for if righteousness
> come by the law, then Christ is dead in vain (Galatians 2:21).

One more passage from the many others:

> For as many as are of the works of the law are under the
> curse: for it is written, Cursed is *every one* that *continueth*
> not in *all things* which are written in the book of the law to do
> them.
> But that no man is justified by the law in the sight of God,
> it is evident: for, The just shall live by faith.
> Christ hath redeemed us from the curse of the law, being
> made a curse for us: for it is written, Cursed is every one
> that hangeth on a tree (Galatians 3:10, 11, 13).

If these verses mean anything at all, they teach the utter hopelessness of being saved by human works or keeping the law of
God. To be saved by the law, the law must be kept *perfectly* and
continuously without interruption. And it applies to *everyone*.
Remember, the Bible says, "Cursed is *every one* that continueth
not in all things."

There are no exceptions, for it says, "*every one*." There must
be unbroken obedience. One single transgression places man
under the law's curse. There must be obedience in *all things*,
without one single interruption or failure. The Bible is crystal-
clear that the law was never given to save a person, never given
to justify the sinner, or sanctify the saint. We repeat, therefore,
God never expected a single sinner to keep the law, for He knew
when He gave the law that this was impossible.

We come, therefore, to the question: Then why did God give
the law anyway, if it could not save man or make him better or
change his heart? This we shall discuss in detail later, but first
we must clear up some misunderstanding about the word, *law*,
itself. What are we to understand by the expressions, "the law of
God" or "the law of Moses"? There are many people who think
only of the Decalogue, the Ten Commandments, whenever they
read the word "law" in the Bible. But the Bible uses the word
"law" to describe different things. Sometimes the word "law"
refers to the whole Word of God. Sometimes the word "law" is
used to distinguish the books of Moses from the rest of the

Scriptures. Jesus speaks of the law and the prophets (Matthew 7:12).

The Jews of Jesus' day divided the Old Testament into: (1) the Law; (2) the Psalms; and (3) the Prophets. The law thus referred to, consists of the five books of Moses. In a general sense the first five books of the Old Testament are referred to as the *law*, as distinguished from the prophetic books of the Old Testament. In a narrower sense, the instructions God gave to Israel through Moses on Mount Sinai are also referred to as the law. This law which God gave to Israel at Mount Sinai after their deliverance from Egypt was a *unit*, yet consisted of different commandments. Most people imagine that the only law Moses brought down from the mountain was the tables of stone —the Ten Commandments—but this was not all. God gave also to Moses the laws concerning the feast days, holy days, sacrifices, offerings, dietary laws, civil laws, and the pattern of the Tabernacle. This law, consisting of all these different commandments and ordinances, which Moses received on the mountain, was given at the same time that he received the Ten Commandments, and is described in detail in Exodus from chapter 20 through 34. All these laws—civil, dietary, sacrificial, and moral— together constitute the books of the law. And this law of God is a unit. There are many commandments but they are all a part of the book of the law.

NOT TWO LAWS

There are also those who, because they do not understand the grace of God and the purpose of the law, make a distinction between the laws of Moses and the law of the Lord, or the law of God. They tell us the *Ten Commandments* are the law of the Lord, while the laws concerning ordinances, offerings, feast days, and the dietary laws are the laws of Moses. They tell us Christ fulfilled the laws of Moses, consisting of ordinances, but His finished work did not include the Ten Commandments. However, the law of Moses and the law of God are one, and to state that the law of Moses was fulfilled and abolished at Calvary, and not the law of the Lord, is a complete misunderstanding of the Bible. The expressions, "law of Moses," and "law of the Lord," are used interchangeably.

THREE BODIES OF COMMANDMENTS

In this very connection we must recognize the three areas covered by the book of the law in its broadest sense. These three parts of the law are:

1. The Commandments of the *moral law* (Exodus 20:1-26).
2. The Judgments (civil laws) (Exodus 21:1-24).
3. The Ordinances (Exodus 24 to 31).

The law of commandments dealt with Israel's moral conduct, and is set forth in the Ten Commandments. The second area (the judgments) dealt with the social conduct of the people, and civil laws for the nation; and the third area (the ordinances) dealt with the ceremonial and religious obligations of the nation of Israel. These included the holy days, the offerings and sacrifices. But all of these are part of THE ONE LAW given by the one same God, at one and the same place, at one and the same time, to one and the same nation by one and the same Moses, and for one and the same purpose.

To show the error of making a difference between the laws of Moses and the law of the Lord contained in the Ten Commandments, we would point out a most convincing fact. The Bible makes no distinction but uses the terms "law of Moses" and "law of God" interchangeably. As an example let me quote from Luke 2:22. It records the observance of the law by Mary, the mother of Jesus:

> And when the days of her [Mary's] purification according to the *law of Moses* were accomplished, they brought him to Jerusalem, to present him to the Lord;
> (As it is written in the *law of the Lord,* Every male that openeth the womb shall be called holy to the Lord;)
> And to offer a sacrifice according to that which is said in the *law of the Lord* . . . (Luke 2:22-24).

Notice in this passage that Mary is said to have taken the baby Jesus to the Temple to present Him to the Lord, in obedience to the *law of the Lord* and to offer a sacrifice according to the *law of the Lord.* Where, I ask you, *where* does it say in the Ten Commandments that she was to bring a sacrifice? That is found in the ceremonial law of Moses, but it is called the law of the Lord. Again in Luke 2:39 we read:

And when they had performed all things according to the
law of the Lord, they returned into Galilee . . . (Luke 2:39).

To make a distinction, therefore, between the laws of Moses
and the law of God or the Lord, for our own convenience, to
prove our own point, is man-made and artificial, and is a violation
of the Scriptures. If Christ fulfilled part of the law, then He fulfilled all of the law, and now the believer is not under the law
but under grace (Romans 6:14). We are delivered from the law
(Romans 7:6), free from the law (Romans 8:2), and dead to the
law (Galatians 2:19).

WHY THEN THE LAW?

Now an important question arises which I am sure has been
suggested by the statement that the law cannot justify, sanctify,
or satisfy. The question is, Then why did God give a law which
no man could keep, but instead only condemned the sinner?
Now Paul, the great exponent of grace, anticipated that question,
and says in Galatians 3:19,

Wherefore then serveth the law? . . .

It was an inevitable question, for Paul had proved in the previous chapters that the law was helpless to save a man or change
a man. And so the question, Then why did God give the law?
What good is it? What purpose does it serve?

Paul immediately gives the answer in one of the most con-
densed, concise, yet comprehensive statements in the Word of
God. What was the reason God gave the law if it cannot save,
justify, sanctify, or satisfy? Read carefully the inspired answer:

    . . . It was *added* because of transgressions, till the seed
should come to whom the promise was made; and it was
ordained by angels in the hand of a mediator (Galatians 3:19).

THREE THINGS STATED

Notice three things which are clearly stated in this answer of
Paul, "It was *added* because of transgressions, till the seed should
come." Notice these three parts of the answer:

1. The beginning of the law—it was added—added, of course,
to something which must have existed before.

2. The end of the law—it was added *till* the seed should come.

The law had not only a beginning but its ministry was *until* the seed should come. It was for a period of time beginning when *it was added,* and lasting *till* the seed should come. Now Paul tells us what he means by the seed. In verse 16 of this chapter he says:

> Now to Abraham and his seed were the promises made. He saith not, And to seeds, as of many; but as of one, And to thy seed, *which is Christ* (Galatians 3:16).

The seed in our verse is Christ, and so we may substitute the word "Christ" for "the seed" and thus we read that the law "was added . . . till Christ should come to whom the promise was made."

The ministry of the law was dispensational. John the Baptist clears up the question as to the length of this dispensation of law. He says in introducing Jesus:

> For the law was given by Moses, but grace and truth came by Jesus Christ (John 1:17).

We shall return to this important passage later on, but we must add a word about the third thing Paul mentions in his answer to "why then the law?" The first was the beginning of the law; the second, the end of the law; and now number 3.

3. The purpose of the law. It was *added* because of transgressions. Literally we may read this, "in order to reveal sin as a transgression." Before the law was given, there was no transgression of the law. There was sin and there was rebellion, but it was not a "transgression" of the law which had not yet been given. Clearly and plainly Paul asserts in Romans 4:15,

> Because the law worketh wrath: for where no law is, there is no transgression (Romans 4:15).

The statement is clear, "before the law came, there was no transgression." We ask the question, Was there then no sin before the law came in? Some folks say that all sin is a transgression of the law. Now transgression of the law, of course, is sin, but before the law came there was sin, even though it was not a transgression of the law, which did not yet exist. Yes, there was sin before the law was given, and sin was just as wicked and wrong then as now, just as horrible and terrible before the law as it was after it came. Paul says clearly,

For until the law sin was in the world: but sin is not imputed [as a transgression] when there is no law (Romans 5:13).

When the law came, it gave to sin a new meaning—it became a transgression of the law. The purpose of the law then was to reveal sin as rebellion against God, as a transgression against better light, for by the law is the knowledge of sin. There is not one verse in the Bible which says that by the law is salvation from sin. This is the first thing a sinner must learn, that no man can be saved by trying to keep the law. The only remedy is to plead guilty before the law, and flee to the Lord Jesus Christ for salvation by the grace of God.

> Not the labors of my hands
> Can fulfill Thy law's demands;
> All for sin could not atone;
> Thou must save, and Thou alone.

Chapter Two

THE BEGINNING OF THE LAW

"Is the Christian under the law?" was already a burning question in the days of Paul; and although the Bible is crystal-clear in the answer that was given under inspiration by the Holy Spirit, that the believer is not under the law, but under grace, yet the proud heart of man will not accept God's grace, but would rather try to save himself by his own goodness and works. And that is just exactly what Satan wants man to do. Satan, the enemy of our souls, wants us to be religious and morally good. He urges men to strive to improve themselves, to try and obey the law, to keep on working and toiling, to be earnest and sincere and religious in all their efforts at keeping the commandments and the sabbath days in an effort to make themselves worthy of God's favor instead of accepting His grace. But Paul says this is another gospel, and just a clever trick of the enemy of our souls to keep us from coming to the Christ of grace as poor, hopeless, helpless sinners. The law, says Paul, was given not to save, but to show the awfulness of sin, and our need of salvation.

This brings us back to the question we raised in our former lesson, and which Paul anticipated in Galatians 3:19,

Wherefore then serveth the law? . . .

Paul immediately answers this vital question, and says:

. . . It was added because of transgressions, till the seed should come . . . (Galatians 3:19).

From this answer we learn that the law had a beginning and it had an ending. It was *added until*. First then we ask *when* was the law added, and to what was it added? When we add something, there must first be something to which it is to be added. When the recipe for baking a cake says "take the yolks of two eggs, and add them to two cups of flour," it is understood that

24

there were first of all two cups of flour to which the rest of the ingredients were to be added. Paul says the law was added. To what was it added? In the context of Galatians 3:19 we find the answer. It was added to the grace of God. Here Paul shows that Abraham lived under grace, and not under law. Notice carefully Paul's argument:

> And this I say, that the covenant, that was confirmed before of God in Christ, [the Abrahamic covenant] the law, [given at Sinai] which was four hundred and thirty years after, cannot disannul, that it should make the promise of none effect.
>
> For if the inheritance be of the law, it is no more of promise: but God gave it to Abraham by promise (Galatians 3:17, 18). *GRACE*

This is a pivotal passage. Paul says that the law was not given until *four hundred and thirty years* after God made His covenant of grace with Abraham. When Abraham lived, there was no written law, but Abraham was under pure grace. There can be no mistaking the words: the law was not given until four hundred and thirty years after God made His covenant promise to Abraham. The covenant of grace with Abraham was unconditional. And then four hundred and thirty years later God *added the law*. Abraham was under grace, Isaac was under grace, Jacob was under grace, the children of Israel were under grace while they were slaves in Egypt. They were delivered from Egypt by grace, they crossed the Red Sea by grace, and then when they reached Mount Sinai, God *added* the law. The law did not supplant grace. It did not take the place of grace. It did not annul the promises of grace. It was *added* and Israel was still under grace when God added the law. Read again Galatians 3:17—the giving of the law did not make void the covenant of grace made to Israel. It was added to grace, so that Israel was under a law which condemned them, but thank God also under grace which made provision for a broken law. If grace had been removed when Israel was given the law, they would all have perished.

WHEN AND WHERE ADDED?

To understand why God added the law to grace, we must see the setting in which the law was given, and the circumstances

bringing it about. We have the detailed record in Exodus 19 and
20. Few Christians are familiar with the circumstances leading
up to the giving of the law. May we suggest that you read and
re-read and study the nineteenth chapter of Exodus. In our
churches we usually hear only the actual Ten Commandments
read, without the all-important verses which precede and follow
the actual declaration of the Decalogue. So turn to the nineteenth chapter of Exodus. Israel had been out of Egypt for
three months (Exodus 19:1). But it was a stormy three months
indeed. Here was a nation delivered from slavery, redeemed
from death, saved by grace, and yet they were scarcely out of
Egypt when they rebelled against God. When they were three
days out of Egypt, we read:

> And the people murmured against Moses, saying, What
> shall we drink? (Exodus 15:24).

God dealt once again in grace and led them (in spite of their
murmurings) to Elim where there were twelve wells of water
and seventy palm trees. But did they appreciate God's grace?
Did they realize the awfulness of their sin of rebellion? Ah, no!
When they left the oasis of Elim they came to Sinai about two
months later. What did they do here? Once more they murmured, and we read:

> And the whole congregation of the children of Israel
> murmured against Moses and Aaron in the wilderness:
> And the children of Israel said unto them, Would to God
> we had died by the hand of the LORD in the land of Egypt,
> when we sat by the flesh pots, and when we did eat bread
> to the full; for ye have brought us forth into this wilderness,
> to kill this whole assembly with hunger (Exodus 16:2, 3).

Can you imagine a people—after having been delivered from
slavery, saved from casting their children into the river, redeemed from Pharaoh's plan to exterminate them—being guilty
of such rebellion against God? Can you imagine this people less
than three months out of bondage, accusing God, as well as
Moses and Aaron, of deliberately bringing them into the wilderness to mercilessly kill them by starvation? They accused Moses
of the sadistic plan of exterminating the people whom he had
first delivered. Why did not God punish them? Why didn't God
send fire from Heaven to devour them? Why did God permit

these delivered slaves to so wickedly accuse Him? Listen to the answer! They were under grace, and not under law! If they had been under law only, God would have damned them into the pit of Hell on the spot, and the glorious history of Israel would never have been written.

GRACE DID ABOUND

Israel was still under the grace of God. God had made His covenant of grace with them through Abraham their father, and so instead of granting their inane request and challenge to God to destroy them, He did the very opposite—He sent them bread from Heaven. It was the bread of God's mercy and grace.

A THIRSTY NATION

They still did not appreciate the grace of God. Soon after this the nation is again accusing God. In Exodus 17 we have the record of the rebellious nation in the wilderness of sin. Again we hear them complaining;

> . . . and the people murmured against Moses, and said, Wherefore is this that thou hast brought us up out of Egypt, to kill us and our children and our cattle with thirst? (Exodus 17:3).

What a terrible accusation against God! But instead of judgment, God answered again in grace and not with the penalty of the law. He caused Moses to smite the rock and the water gushed forth. All this happened within three months after they had seen the marvelous salvation of the Lord. What was wrong with this people anyway? The answer is simple. They did not know or recognize the gravity, the seriousness of their sin. They did not understand the character and nature of sin. They knew not the penalty of their rebellion. They did not appreciate the fact that it was God's mercy and grace that had spared them. They were not conscious of the greatness of their sin and their inability to live a life pleasing to God. They thought they deserved better treatment from God. They imagined that they were able to do God's will perfectly. It was not their fault (they reasoned) that they thirsted and hungered—it was God's fault. In brief, they did not know the seriousness and gravity of sin. For this reason God is now going to give Israel a law, a perfect law, to reveal to them what sin really is.

THE BACKGROUND

It is with this background of murmuring, rebellion, and ingratitude that God is to give the law on Mount Sinai to Israel. God calls Moses into the mountain, and gives him a message for Israel. We read in Exodus 19:3,

> . . . Thus shalt thou say to the house of Jacob, and tell the children of Israel [notice the message];
> Ye have seen what I did unto the Egyptians, and how I bare you on eagles' wings, and brought you unto myself (Exodus 19:3, 4).

Observe carefully what God reminds them of before He gives them the tables of the Ten Commandments. He reminds them that they were under grace. Everything that had happened to them, their deliverance from the Egypt of slavery and death was the undeserved grace of God. If God had dealt with them in justice according to the law, they would have perished. So the Lord reminds them, before they make the mistake of choosing *law* over grace, how that all God's blessings were of grace. And having reminded them of their position under grace, the Lord adds the word "*IF.*" God's grace was unconditional, but God now adds conditions, and says:

> Now therefore, *if* ye will obey my voice indeed, and keep my covenant, then ye shall be a peculiar treasure unto me above all people: for all the earth is mine (Exodus 19:5).

God now proposes a new thing—*conditional blessing.* He says He will do something for them upon condition of their obedience. If they will *obey* God's voice and *keep* God's covenant, then the Lord will bless them.

How blind man is! The history of the past three months out of Egypt had proven that Israel could not *obey* God perfectly; they had *not* kept God's covenant perfectly. They had failed again and again and again, but the grace of God had forgiven them again and again and again. Apparently they did not realize the real gravity of their sin. They did not appreciate grace, but believed they could do anything the Lord required.

One would have thought that when God suggests the giving of the law and making their blessings conditional upon their perfect obedience, they would have cried out, "Oh no, Moses. Oh, no! Go back up the mountain to the LORD and tell him we do not want to be put under a law which we cannot keep; we don't want His blessings to be dependent upon our perfect obedience, our merit, our works. We are unworthy, we are unable to do God's will perfectly. Tell the Lord we want to remain under grace." But though almost unbelievable, the answer of Israel is the exact opposite. Listen to Israel's answer to God's *if*:

> And all the people answered together, and said, *All that the LORD hath spoken we will do.* And Moses returned the words of the people unto the LORD (Exodus 19:8).

Poor, foolish Israel! Poor, blinded people! They thought they could keep God's commandments, and so they say, "*All* that the Lord commands we will *do*." Yes, we will *do*! *Do*! *Do*! Instead, they ought to have said, "Oh, God, we need grace and mercy—not law, for we have already proven we cannot obey Thee and keep Thy word perfectly." They chose conditional blessings (*if*) and chose to be placed under the law, for they were confident that they were able to keep any law which God gave them. And so God seems to say, You think you can keep My Commandments? Well, I'll give you a law. I'll give you a set of rules, which will be the most perfect expression of the will of God, a perfect revelation of God's holiness, the perfect requirements for earning or meriting the blessing of God. God is now to give them a law which will reveal the true nature of sin, and the requirements for complete, continuous, uninterrupted obedience, and which will show the inability of Israel to keep it. God seems to say, if you think you can keep my commandments, here they are. See what you can do with them.

GOD'S CHANGE OF ATTITUDE

Moses goes up to God and brings Israel's message, "All that God requires, we are able to do." So the Lord, to show them the utter folly of their ignorant notion that they could *do what* He commanded, now will give to them a law which would convince them of the very opposite—that man cannot be saved by keeping the law, but still needs the grace of God. This then is the background for the giving of the law—ending with "all that God demands we will do." Israel chooses *law* instead of grace, and immediately God's whole attitude to Israel changes. God now hides His face and comes in a thick cloud (Exodus 19:9), and the giving of the law is accompanied by prohibitions, threatenings, penalties of death, ceremonialism, thunders, lightnings, the whole mountain smoking, and there is a terrible earthquake. In this setting of judgment God now gives the law. May we suggest that you read carefully, very carefully, the description of the giving of the law as recorded in Exodus 19: 9-24. It is a scene of judgment, threatenings and darkness. It is the picture of the ministry of the law. The law could only demonstrate God's displeasure upon sin, but could not save from sin.

Chapter Three

THE BACKGROUND OF THE LAW

If you want to read a hair-raising, frightening, dramatic story of dreadful convulsions of nature, let me suggest the account of the giving of the law of the Ten Commandments on Mount Sinai. In Exodus 19 we read:

> And it came to pass on the third day in the morning, that there were thunders and lightnings, and a thick cloud upon the mount, and the voice of the trumpet exceeding loud; so that all the people that was in the camp trembled. And mount Sinai was altogether on a smoke, because the LORD descended upon it in fire: and the smoke thereof ascended as the smoke of a furnace, and the whole mount quaked greatly (Exodus 19:16, 18).

In this dramatic setting God gave to Israel His holy law of commandments. It is a climactic change in God's approach to the nation. Before this, God had dealt in grace and mercy, but Israel did not appreciate God's grace, was not conscious of the meaning of God's goodness and mercy, and imagined that they could by their own work and obedience please God. When Moses proposed placing them under law, they had said, "All that the Lord hath spoken we will do. So the Lord says, "You need to learn that you cannot do it at all." I'll give you a law, a perfect law. See if you can keep it." Notice the immediate change in the tone of Jehovah to Israel after they had declared they did not want grace, for they could *do* it themselves, and keep the law. Listen to the result:

> And the LORD said unto Moses, Lo, I come unto thee in a thick cloud . . . (Exodus 19:9).

Clouds now appear, hiding God's face. Next the Lord says:

> . . . Go unto the people, and sanctify [separate] them to day and to morrow, and let them wash their clothes (Exodus 19:10).

Here is the law for you. It comes with ceremonialism, observances, and places a barrier between God and His people. Now follow the rest of the record:

> And thou shalt set bounds unto the people round about, saying, Take heed to yourselves, that ye go not up into the mount, or touch the border of it: whosoever toucheth the mount shall be surely put to death (Exodus 19:12).

He shall be put to death! The law has come and is the minister of death. Come not near, *lest ye die.* How differently grace pleads:

> Come unto me, all ye that labour and are heavy laden, and I will give you rest (Matthew 11:28).

And "him that cometh to me I will in no wise cast out" (John 6:37). "Let him that is athirst *come,* and take the water of life freely" (Revelation 22:17). That is the language of grace. But the law says, "Set bounds, let them not come near, lest they die"—*keep away.* The law kills; grace makes alive.

> There shall not an hand touch it, but he *shall surely be stoned, or shot through;* whether it be beast or man, *it shall not live . . .* (Exodus 19:13).

To be overtaken in the fault of touching the mount, meant death. That was *law.* But when grace speaks it says, "Brethren, if a man be overtaken in a fault, ye which are spiritual, *restore such an one*" (Galatians 6:1). That is grace. The two are not only different, but work the opposite in the dealing with sin.

Then in the following two verses (14 and 15), there is added still more ceremonialism, and the Israelites are commanded not *to come at their wives.* But grace says, "Marriage is honourable in all, and the bed undefiled" (Hebrews 13:4). And so we might go on to show the contrast of law and grace. In the balance of the nineteenth chapter of Exodus we have a further picture of the effect of the law, in the smoke, the trembling of the mount, and the fear of the people. What a picture of what the law does! It brings fear and puts men under bondage, and it is the "yoke" which the New Testament says neither you nor your fathers were able to bear (Acts 15:10).

Then follows the twentieth chapter with the law given on the tables of stone. In the first two verses (the prologue) God again reminds them of the fact that it is the same God who by grace led them out of Egypt, who is now giving them at their own request, the law. Listen to the words:

> And God spake all these words, saying,
> I am the LORD thy God, which have brought thee out of the land of Egypt, out of the house of bondage (Exodus 20:1, 2).

He reminds them of the fact that they were under grace, before He gives them the law. It is a biting reminder and a sharp rebuke for their presumptuousness in saying, "All that the Lord hath spoken we will *do*." Now then, O children of Israel, if you want to be saved by a code of *do's*, here it is, and He gives the law—a series of commands and prohibitions: *thou shalt not, thou shalt not, thou shalt not,* and *thou shalt, thou shalt,* etc. Here is law for you. Live up to that if you can. God gave them a law, and a good law it was. There could be no better. It was a perfect law, a good law; and because the law is perfect and just, it *must punish all who made even the slightest breach of its demands.*

> . . . Cursed is *every* one that *continueth not* in *all* things which are written in the book of the law to *do* them (Galatians 3:10).

God gave them the law—the law which cursed and condemned. Israel had refused grace, so the law *was added*—the law that could not save; the law that was the ministry of death; the law that condemned all who tried to be saved by its works. Then see the result in the verses that follow the giving of the law. These verses are seldom if ever read in those churches where the law is read every Sunday morning. But it belongs with it. Add the thunderings and the lightnings and the smoke and the trembling mount, and the still more trembling people crying,

> . . . Speak thou with us, and we will hear: but let not God speak with us, lest we die (Exodus 20:19).

If you want to cling to the law, then take all the law and all the trimmings that go with it. Here then we have seen the beginning of the law amid the thunders of judgment and condemnation. It was to demonstrate that man cannot be saved by *doing.* The law could not give peace, but only gender fear;

not bring us to God but separate us from Him instead. The law God gave was perfect; therefore imperfect man cannot keep it; it is holy, and therefore sinful men are condemned by it. It was a just law, and therefore must punish the transgressor.

Then if man cannot be saved by keeping the law, how can he be saved? Only by grace. Under this grace Israel was delivered from Egypt. And this grace remained, as the only hope of Israel, even after God gave them the law. The law did not take the place of grace. Grace was not removed to make place for the law. No, indeed, the grace of God remained, for if Israel had been placed simply under the law, they would have perished immediately.

This is the force of the words of Paul in answer to the question, "Wherefore then serveth the law?" We have seen the answer—*it was added*; added to grace. For over sixteen hundred years Israel was under that perfect law, yet not *one* single Israelite was ever saved by keeping that law, but they ended up after sixteen hundred years, committing the capital crime of the universe by nailing to the cross the only Man who ever did keep the law of God perfectly—even Jesus Christ. The law was given to prove that man cannot keep the law to be saved, and thus make him willing to receive the grace of God, without the works of the law. Here then we have the *beginning* of the law. It was added at Sinai, not to replace grace, but added to grace. Every Israelite believer during the entire age of the law from Sinai to Calvary was still saved by grace. We turn now to the *end* of the law, for Paul says:

> . . . It [the law] was added . . . till the seed should come (Galatians 3:19).

The meaning of the seed is explained in Galatians 3:16,

> Now to Abraham and his seed were the promises made. He saith not, And to seeds, as of many; but as of one, And to thy seed, *which is Christ* (Galatians 3:16).

At Calvary the age of law ended. Jesus had kept its precepts perfectly for thirty-three years and then went as the perfect Man, the last Adam, to Calvary and paid the penalty of the broken law, and cried, "*It is finished.*" And to prove He had fully paid the penalty which was *death*, He arose the third day from the tomb.

As a result the believer today is "free from the law" (Romans 8:2); delivered from the law" (Romans 7:6); and "dead to the law" (Galatians 2:19). The law is not dead, but we are dead to the law. The law is very much alive. It is still the expression of God's perfect holiness and judgment upon the sinner. But for the believer the penalty has been borne by Christ, and now we serve the Lord, not out of fear of judgment and punishment, but because of love for our Saviour for such a great salvation.

Now I anticipate that someone will say, "Do we not need the law to show us the awfulness of sin?" Yes, the law reveals sin as a transgression. However, this is not the full answer. On the surface it would seem that we would need the law, but listen, friend, we have something else which shows and reveals the terribleness of human nature like no law ever could. We have the cross. Look at that cross and see what sin did to Him. Do you want a picture of man's corrupt nature? Then see that howling mob at the foot of the cross. Do you want a picture of what sin is and what it will do? Then come with me from Sinai, and go to Calvary. Oh, there we see sin as it is. And it was a nation that had boasted in the law for sixteen hundred years and yet at the end of it all, they nailed the Son of God to the tree.

See *Him* as He grovels in the Garden, the great drops of bloody sweat pouring upon the ground. What drove Him there? It was our sins. See Him as He looks into the cup that His Father gave Him. The cup into which all your sins and failures, your lyings and adulteries had been squeezed, until they were the very quintessence of the dregs of Hell, His back grooved with the cruel lashes, His brow pierced with cruel thorns. See Him as they spit upon Him and strike Him in the face, as they rudely pluck the hairs from His blessed cheek. Follow Him, as they lead Him to Calvary. See Him there with sunken eyes and heaving chest, as "God makes him to be sin for us who knew no sin, that we might be made the righteousness of God in him." Hear Him as He sends that soul-piercing cry to Heaven, "*My God, my God, why* hast *thou* forsaken Me?" See Him as He breathes His last. The sweet frame quivers for a moment, the hollow eyes stare once more with pity, as He utters the "finis cry"—*it is finished.* Oh, friend, there you can see what sin does, and if you cannot see it there, surely there is no law that can reveal it unto you. The law ceased there at Calvary for the believer, because it was superseded by something that would show the awfulness of sin as no law, however perfect, ever could show.

Remember, He was *innocent.* He was the same One who made the world. He said, "Before the world was, I am." He was in the beginning with the Father. Yet see what sin did to Him. There you have the picture of naked sin in all its horror. On that cross we see not only sin, but we see the remedy as well. There the law with its curse came to an end, having done its work and having done it perfectly. The man or the woman who still can cling to the law in this day and age, has never yet seen the cross in its full light of redemption. If a vision of the cross of Calvary will not convince a man of sin, the law never will. Anyone who can stand there and see what his miserable sins have done to the Son of God and not be moved by it, need never expect to be moved by the law. The preaching of the law will never save a soul until the cross is put in its place. Jesus said not, "If the *law* be lifted up" but "If I be lifted up, I will draw all men unto me." Paul did not say, "God forbid that I should glory, save in the law of Moses" but "God forbid that I should glory, save in the *cross* of our Lord Jesus Christ." Preaching law may bring fear and trembling, and may fill the church with trembling church members, but the preaching of the cross is the power of God unto *salvation.*

Yes, you can go to the law, the eternal expression of what God expects a sinner to do, if he wants to be saved by his own work and righteousness; but you must turn from your own efforts to the finished work of Christ on the cross if you are to be saved. The law can show you your sinfulness, but cannot take away your sin. This is the work of grace. This is the way of salvation.

Chapter Four

SIN AS A TRANSGRESSION OF THE LAW

Is the believer under the law? This was already a burning question in the days of Paul; and while the Bible gives its clear and unmistakable answer, it is still being asked by thousands of earnest, sincere, but mistaken, believers. Some even say, Yes, we are under the law for salvation. If we are to be saved, we must do so by keeping the law. But the Bible says:

> Knowing that a man is not justified by the works of the law, but by the faith of Jesus Christ, even we have believed in Jesus Christ, that we might be justified by the faith of Christ, and not by the works of the law: for by the works of the law shall no flesh be justified (Galatians 2:16).

Then there are others who teach that we are saved by grace, but then after that we are kept saved by keeping the law. But the Bible says:

> . . . Cursed is every one that continueth not in all things which are written in the book of the law to do them (Galatians 3:10).

If we are to be kept by the law, our obedience must be perfect, continuous and uninterrupted. And this brings us right back to that vital question with which we began this series of messages. The question is then, What is the law good for? Why was it given? What did it accomplish? If it cannot save a man, or keep a believer, or make a person better, but only punish him, then what is the purpose of the law? That is, we repeat, the question, or as Paul puts it:

> Wherefore then serveth the law? (Galatians 3:19).

The answer is, "It was added because of transgressions." In other words, it was added to reveal sin as a transgression against God. Before the law was given, there was sin in the world, but

37

there was no transgression of the law. This is made clear by Paul in Romans:

> For the promise, that he should be the heir of the world, was not to Abraham, or to his seed, *through the law, but through the righteousness of faith.*
> For if they which are of the law be heirs, faith is made void, and the promise made of none effect:
> Because the law worketh wrath: for *where no law is, there is no transgression* (Romans 4:13-15).

There is no mistaking these words, "where no law is, there is no transgression." We repeat, sin was in the world before the law was given, and the penalty of sin was death. How clearly Paul states it in Romans:

> Wherefore, as by one man sin entered into the world, and death by sin; and so death passed upon all men, for that all have sinned:
> (For until the law sin was in the world: but sin is not imputed [that is, as a transgression] when there is no law. . . . (Romans 5:12, 13).

In order to show man the real nature of sin, which he did not realize, God gave him the law. There are three words in the Hebrew for "sin." The most common word is *hattah* and means literally, "missing the mark." God has placed a target, as it were, for man to shoot at. If he misses, he has failed of a perfect score. He has missed the mark, and an inch is as good as a mile. The target which God has given may be said to be the law. It is the perfect expression of His perfect will. To fail to make a bull's eye by a perfect hit, is missing the mark. To miss by a hair makes one a loser. The target which God sets up—the law—is so high that sinful man cannot begin to live up to it. It must be a perfect hit. Coming close will not do, for the Word says (and we repeat it over and over),

> . . . Cursed is every one that continueth not in *all* things which are written in the book of the law to do them (Galatians 3:10).

The requirement is absolute—it must be perfect obedience; it must be continuous obedience; it must be uninterrupted. James says:

For whosoever shall keep the whole law, and yet offend in one point, he is guilty of all (James 2:10).

The law is a unit. Like a chain, it consists of different links, but it is still one chain, and it takes only one broken link to break the chain. Do not suppose that "almost" keeping the law is enough, that keeping all the commandments except one, will do; or keeping it all your life, except for one minute, can satisfy its demands. No, it must be a bull's eye—perfect obedience. Sin, then, is "coming short" of God's perfect demands. A second word for sin is *avon* and means, "a flaw or irregularity." It is a deviation from a straight line, and therefore suggests crookedness. The law demands that we walk in a perfectly straight line, according to its demands of perfection, and one misstep makes us sinners. The slightest deviation from the straight line of God's law places us under judgment.

TRANSGRESSION

The third word for sin is *pesha*, and it is translated "transgression." It means to trespass upon forbidden ground. It means crossing a line or violating a boundary. The law sets up a boundary of holiness and perfection. It demands of man that he shall not cross the line which God has set. It is like the signs we see along the roadside—"Private Property—Do Not Trespass—Keep Out—This means you!" Now if there is no fence, or a plain line to show the limits of the forbidden property, one cannot know when he is trespassing. Before the law came, sin was sin, to be sure, but the line had not been clearly drawn—no fence had been erected to show the exact limit of the forbidden ground. Then God put up a fence, in giving Israel the law of the Ten Commandments. It defined the exact limits, and to go beyond this was sin. Before the law, sin was sin, but it was not a transgression of the law. We have dwelt on this aspect of the matter of sin and the law because certain legalistic law-teachers continually quote the verse:

. . . for sin is the transgression of the law (I John 3:4).

This verse is quoted as though all sin is transgression of the law. But transgression, positive disobedience to the law, is only one aspect of sin. There is also a negative aspect of sin: *coming short* of the demands of the law. Sins of *omission* are as much sins as sins of ~~commission~~. It is as much a sin to "fail to do good", ~~as to be guilty of doing evil~~. And so we call your attention to the complete verse in I John 3. It not only says, "For sin is the transgression of the law," but it is preceded by the first part of the same verse:

> Whosoever committeth sin transgresseth *also* the law (I John 3:4)..

Sin was not always a transgression, but it was always sin, even before the law. So remember that sin is a transgression only since the giving of the law, but it is more than a transgression. Transgression is the legal definition of sin. Sin was always morally wrong, but not legally. This the law brought about. We repeat, a thing may be morally wrong, but not be the breaking of any law.

SLAVERY

Consider an illustration. Up until about a hundred years ago it was perfectly legal to own and traffic in slaves in the United States of America. You could own slaves, buy them, sell them, and treat them in any way you pleased. It was perfectly legal. It was not a transgression of any law on our books. Then came the emancipation declaration, and the passage of laws against slavery with its appropriate penalties and punishments. And now it became legally wrong, and a crime to traffic in slavery. Now slavery was always wrong, but it was not always illegal. It was not a breaking of any law. But now the law enters and it becomes a transgression of that law. We repeat, slavery was just as wrong before the laws were passed as after. It was always morally wrong. When the law came, it did not change the nature of the practice or affect the moral question of slavery, but it only made it illegal as well as immoral.

Or take another illustration. Before World War I, it was not a transgression of the law to make, buy, sell, and drink liquor and alcoholic intoxicants. But after that war prohibition came in, making the manufacture, selling, and buying of whiskey, beer, and wine for beverage purposes illegal and punishable by fines and imprisonment. And then to America's everlasting shame, the 18th Amendment was repealed and the liquor traffic once more became legal. The law against liquor was no more. Now, passing the law and repealing the law did not affect by one iota the rightness or the wrongness of the liquor traffic. It was morally wrong during prohibition, and it was legally wrong as well, for it was a transgression of the law. But the liquor traffic today, although legalized, is still just as morally wrong, wicked, inexcusable, and damning in its results as when it was illegal in those prohibition days. The law cannot change the moral nature of a thing that is intrinsically wrong.

Not too many years ago there were no laws to prevent child labor, sweat shops, and starvation wages. Of course, it was morally wrong, but it was not illegal. There were no laws prohibiting the practice, and where no law is, there is no transgression. Then the law entered, and that which was always morally wrong also became legally wrong. We have dwelt on this aspect of transgression to show that we cannot legislate morality. We cannot change the hearts of men by laws and regulations.

LAW CANNOT CHANGE THE HEART

The law can restrain and discourage sin, but it cannot remove the desire to sin. If the penalty for an infraction of the law is made severe enough, it will inhibit and reduce infraction of the law, but cannot change the desire. Men will continue to break the law if they can do so without danger of detection or prosecution. Prohibition could forbid the manufacture and use of intoxicants, but it did not stop it or change man's desire for it. It merely drove it underground in an effort to escape the penalty of the law. The law prohibiting liquor under penalty might stop the practice for some, but it could not stop their thirst, and the law failed to put an end to the perverted appetites of men, and it blossomed out in an age of bootlegging, "blind pigs," and flagrant violations.

NEED A CHANGE OF HEART

Now all of this is not because laws are not good and just and right. In the kind of a world we are living, we need laws—to restrain, to inhibit, to discourage crime—but it takes more than laws to change the heart of man. There are some things the law cannot do. It cannot do a single thing to improve the sinful heart of man. Its very purpose was to prove that we cannot legislate goodness. We cannot pass any laws which will make

us love our neighbor or seek to please God. The Apostle Paul
sums it all up when he says in Romans,

> For what the law could *not* do, in that [because] it was
> weak through the flesh, God sending his own Son in the like-
> ness of sinful flesh, and for sin, condemned sin in the flesh:
> That the righteousness of the law might be fulfilled *in*
> us, who walk not after the flesh, but after the Spirit (Romans
> 8:3, 4).

"For what the law could not do," says Paul. This comes as
quite a surprise, I am sure, to many who had the mistaken
notion that the keeping of the law could save a person. And
indeed it is true that if a person could be found who kept the
law of God flawlessly, perfectly, and continuously all his life, he
could claim salvation on the basis of his perfect, sinless holiness,
and keeping of the law. But such a person never lived. We are
born with Adam's sin imputed to us, and under the sentence of
death. David says,

> Behold, I was shapen in iniquity; and in sin did my
> mother conceive me (Psalm 51:5).

In I Kings 8:46 we read,

> . . . for there is no man that sinneth not . . .

Solomon tells us that,

> An high look, and a proud heart, and the plowing of the
> wicked, is sin (Proverbs 21:4).

And in verse 9 of chapter 24, he tells us:

> The thought of foolishness is sin . . . (Proverbs 24:9).

David says in Psalm 14:

> The LORD looked down from heaven upon the children
> of men, to see if there were *any* that did understand, and
> seek God (Psalm 14:2).

And what did the Lord find as He looked down upon the
children of men? Listen to it:

> They are all gone aside, they are all together become
> filthy: there is *none* that doeth good, no, not one (Psalm
> 14:3).

God says no man can be saved by his good works, no one can be saved by keeping the law. The only hope is the grace of God. To be saved you must *first* acknowledge your total depravity, your complete inability to please God by the works of the law, and then abandoning all hope of saving yourself, throw yourself upon the mercy and grace of God, and say:

> Rock of ages, cleft for me,
> Let me hide myself in Thee;
> Let the water and the blood,
> From Thy wounded side which flowed,
> Be of sin the double cure,
> Cleanse me from its guilt and power.
>
> Not the labors of my hands
> Can fulfill Thy law's demands;
> Could my zeal no respite know,
> Could my tears forever flow,
> All for sin could not atone;
> Thou must save, and Thou alone.

This is your only hope. Abandon all hope in self, and say:

> Just as I am, without one plea,
> But that Thy blood was shed for me,
> And that Thou bidd'st me come to Thee,
> O Lamb of God, I come! I come!

Chapter Five

DELIVERANCE FROM THE LAW

Wherefore then serveth the law? It was added because of
transgressions, till the seed should come . . . (Galatians
3:19).

Almost 3500 years ago God gave to Israel, at Mount Sinai,
two tables of a law, which no one since then has ever kept
perfectly. This law was the faultless expression of the holy will
of God, and sinful man was unable to keep it. Some 1500 years
after God gave this law to Israel there had not been one single
person who could claim complete obedience to this law. This
made all men law-breakers, for one transgression was enough to
bring a person under its curse. We repeat without apology, the
all-inclusive indictment of the Apostle Paul:

For as many as are of the works of the law are under
the curse: for it is written, Cursed is *every one* that *continueth* not in *all* things which are written in the book of
the law to do them (Galatians 3:10).

This verse universally and individually condemns every man,
for the demands of this law are entirely out of reach of the best
human who ever lived. It was impossible for a sinner born with
a depraved heart to please God by obedience to His perfect,
holy law. Again and again the Bible states that no flesh can be
justified by the works of the law. Paul says in Galatians that,

. . . if there had been a law given which could have given
life, verily righteousness should have been by the law.
But the scripture hath concluded all under sin . . . (Galatians 3:21, 22).

It is well to ponder those words: If it were possible for a
sinner to have made himself acceptable in the sight of God by a
life of perfect obedience to God's law, then there would have
been no need, no occasion, for the grace and the mercy of God.

It would have made the death of Christ wholly unnecessary. For this reason Paul says,

> I do not frustrate the grace of God: for if righteousness come by the law, then Christ is dead in vain (Galatians 2:21).

What a charge to hurl against a righteous God! If it were possible for man to attain righteousness by keeping the law, then God made a colossal mistake in sending His Son to die on the cross. We repeat, if it were possible for man to be saved by his own merit, works, and obedience to God's law, then there was no need of sacrificing the Son of God to save those who were perfectly able to save themselves. This is the force of these words:

> . . . if righteousness come by the law, *then Christ is dead in vain* (Galatians 2:21).

Then the death of Christ on the cross was wholly unnecessary and uncalled for. The question therefore arises over and over again: If the law could neither justify, sanctify, or satisfy, then why did God give a law which He knew no one would be able to keep? Is it not debasing to the law to say that it could not save the sinner? What is wrong with the perfect law of God, if it can do absolutely nothing for the sinner as to obtaining salvation? Listen! There is nothing wrong with the law. The trouble is with the sinner. The standard of the law is perfection and holiness. Paul says in Romans 7,

> Wherefore the law is holy, and the commandment holy, and just, and good (Romans 7:12).

The law is holy; therefore unholy sinners cannot keep it. The law is *just*; therefore it condemns the unjust sinner. The law is good; therefore it condemns the evil, wicked heart of the natural man. It was given to reveal the sinfulness of sin, not to enable man to get rid of his sin. The law makes us *see* sin, but it cannot take away sin. It was Moody who used the illustration of the mirror. He compared the law of God to a mirror in which he might behold himself as he really is. Without a mirror one is unable to have an accurate picture of himself. No one has ever seen his own face. Because our eyes are set back in sockets and can only look forward and sideways, but not backward, no one has ever seen his own face. When you look in a mirror, you do not see your face; you see only the reflection of it. A photograph is a picture of your face, but you don't actually see your face. Now a perfect mirror will give a perfect reflection. Without a mirror one might imagine his face to be perfectly clean, but looking in the mirror he sees that it is dirty, soiled and even filthy.

Before God gave His holy law, man was unable to see just how he actually looked in the sight of God. He knew something was wrong, for his conscience told him that. But he had no idea of just how sinful and filthy he really was. He had no conception of the real sinfulness of sin. At Sinai, at the giving of the law, they said, "All that the Lord hath said, we will *do*." Poor, blinded, deluded souls! They had no realization of how depraved they were, how utterly helpless to keep the law which they were about to receive. So, in order to show them their real condition, God gave them a perfect law, as the standard of God's requirements for holiness. It was a revelation of how far short they had come before God. The law then, instead of showing them how good they were, or how good they should be, or how good they *might* be by obedience to the law, only increased the sinfulness of sin. The Apostle Paul had to learn by experience this great lesson, that the law, instead of giving life, was a minister of death. Before his conversion, Paul was a zealous law-keeper. As touching the outward observance of the law, he was blameless. No one could point the finger of accusation at him. And then Paul came face to face with Jesus Christ, and in a flash Paul saw that all his righteousness which he claimed under the law was only filthy rags, and he testifies in Romans 7:10,

> And the commandment, which was ordained to life, I found to be unto death (Romans 7:10).

Paul found that the law which he so diligently sought to keep in order to earn salvation, was instead his executioner, and condemned him to death. He says that the law, instead of giving life, *slew him*:

> For sin, taking occasion by the commandment, deceived me [sin deceived me], and by it [the commandment or the law] slew me (Romans 7:11).

And it is then that Paul realized the high standard of God's law and adds in verse 12:

Wherefore the law is holy, and the commandment holy, and just, and good (Romans 7:12).

The purpose of the law was to show the real, the awful nature of sin. It did not cause sin, but it revealed the true nature of sin. Continuing Paul's argument in Romans 7 we read:

Was then that which is good made death unto me? [Is the law the cause of sin?] God forbid. But sin, that it might appear sin, working death in me by that which is good; that sin by the commandment might become exceeding sinful (Romans 7:13).

Notice that last phrase, *that sin by the commandment might become exceeding sinful.*

Before the law, man might claim ignorance of God's perfect will, but once the law came, there was no longer any self-justification. Paul states the same truth in Romans 5:20,

Moreover the law entered, that the offence might abound (Romans 5:20).

The law then became like a mirror to reveal the true condition of the sinner as he is. Without the mirror man did not see himself as he really is. But that is all a mirror can do—show the filthiness of the face, and the need for cleansing. It cannot do the washing. To take the mirror and try to use it for a washcloth will only smear the dirt and spread it all over your face. To rub the mirror over your soiled complexion will only make matters worse. We must turn from the mirror to soap and water. So, too, with the ministry of the law—it was given to show man his true condition and his need for cleansing, but beyond this it cannot go. We must now turn to the grace of God and in true repentance and confession of our guilt seek for cleansing by the water of the Word and the regenerating power of the Holy Spirit. We repeat and shall repeat and repeat: the ministry of the law is *not to save*, but to show the *need of salvation*. When God gave the law to Israel, they did not yet know the gravity of their sin. They imagined they were capable and able to earn and merit the favor of God by their own behavior and good works. So God gave them a set of conditions, a set of rules, to be observed if they were to merit God's favor. For sixteen hundred years Israel lived under this law, and yet in all those sixteen hundred years, *not one* single Israelite was saved by keeping that law. Without exception, all who were saved were saved *by grace*, through faith in God's atoning sacrifice. When God gave the law on Mount Sinai, He also gave the pattern of the Tabernacle and the ordinances for the bloody sacrifices. These sacrifices and the Tabernacle pointed to the coming Redeemer. Had God given only the law on Sinai, without God's provisions for pardon in the pattern of the Tabernacle with its bloody atoning sacrifices, not a single Israelite would have been saved.

FROM SINAI TO CALVARY

To the believer who comes to Christ and abandons all hope of saving himself, Christ becomes the end of the law. Perfect obedience to the law is not to him the condition of salvation, but confession of failure and acceptance of grace result in his justification.

> For Christ is the end of the law for righteousness to every one that believeth (Romans 10:4).

Notice well, "Christ is the end of the law *for righteousness*" to the believer. He does not say that the law ceases to exist, but for the believer the law is ended as a means of obtaining righteousness through obedience to it. He is now saved by grace. So today we are not under law, but under grace. The believer is not under the law, its threatenings, or its penalties. We are "dead to the law" (Galatians 2:19), free from the law, and delivered from the law.

> Free from the law, O happy condition!
> Jesus has died, and there is remission;
> Cursed by the law, Ruined by the fall,
> Christ hath redeemed us, Once for all.
>
> Once for all, O sinner, receive it;
> Once for all; O doubter, believe it;
> Look to the Cross, your burden will fall,
> Christ hath redeemed us, Once for all.
> —P. P. Bliss, alt.

With the death and resurrection of Christ, the dispensation of law ended, and when Jesus cried, "It is finished," He had met all the demands of the holy law, paid its penalty, and to us who believe, "the righteousness of the law is imputed to us and fulfilled *in* us."

But someone will ask the question, Do we not need the law today to show us what sin really is? My friend, may I ask you honestly, do we need to go to the law to see what sin is and does? To be sure, the law still stands to condemn the sinner, but we now have a much more convincing demonstration of the true nature of sin. It is seen not at Sinai, but at Calvary. After sixteen hundred years of the thunderings of the law, not one single individual to whom the law was given ever kept it, but instead at the end of those sixteen hundred years they committed the capital crime of the ages by nailing the *only One* who ever kept the law perfectly, to the cross of Calvary and condemned Him to die as a criminal and a law-breaker. Mark this fact well—after living for centuries under the law, they ended up by committing the crime of all crimes, crucifying the Son of God. Ah, my friend, if you really want to see what sin is in all its naked depravity, then come with me to Calvary. See the perfect, sinless Son of God bleeding, dying in agony and shame, because of *our sin*. There is the picture of sin. There we see what sin really is, and what sin deserves, for He bore our sin on that cross. If you want to know what sin is, go to that scene at Calvary. You will never truly repent of your sin until you see what your sin did to the Saviour on the cross.

I was born and raised in a church where the law of the Ten Commandments was read at every Sunday morning service. It was a requirement. It spoke to me of condemnation and judgment but it never changed my heart. Then one day I came face to face with Calvary and the grace of God, and in one minute, one look at Him melted my stony heart which for thirty-one years had resisted the threatenings of the law. One moment at Calvary did what years of living in the shadow of Sinai under the thunderings of the law could not do. Oh, turn from your own efforts, and confess that you are a guilty sinner, who has broken every law of God, and turn to the Christ of Calvary for grace and mercy, and find His peace.

> I saw One hanging on a tree,
> In agony and blood.
> He fixed His loving eyes on me,
> As near His cross I stood.

Chapter Six

THE POWER OF THE LAW

Is the believer in Christ under law or under grace? This is the question we discussed in the previous series of messages on LAW OR GRACE. From the days of the apostles there have been many views held by various groups; and though the Bible is crystal-clear on the subject, the different interpretations persist, and there are still the widest differences of opinion on the matter. In general, we can classify the errors concerning law and grace under three heads. There are three erroneous interpretations proposed by three schools of thought. The first of these is *legalism*. This interpretation teaches that we are saved by our own works, by keeping the law, and observing the Ten Commandments. This error was already present even before the days of the apostles, and the Holy Spirit inspired the Apostle Paul to write one whole epistle to refute this gross soul-destroying error. It is the epistle to the Romans. The entire thrust of Romans is simply this: we are saved by grace wholly apart from the works of the law. He gives us the conclusion of his whole argument in that well-known verse:

Therefore we conclude that a man is justified by faith without the deeds of the law (Romans 3:28).

The second error with regard to the ministry of the law is called *antinomianism*, which is the exact opposite of legalism. The theological term "antinomianism" comes from two words *anti* (against) and *nomos* (the law), and means literally, "against the law." It teaches that since we are saved by grace, it makes no difference how a person lives or behaves. This is also a soul-destroying error, and again the Holy Spirit has devoted one whole book in the New Testament to refute this doctrine of antinomianism. This is the epistle of James, in which the Lord sets forth the fact that although we are delivered from the law of commandments by the work of Christ, we are not then left without law, and become lawless, but instead we are placed

50

under a new law, the law of a new life, called the royal law of liberty. It is the law of love and gratitude in response to our salvation by grace alone. It teaches that while works have no part in obtaining or retaining salvation, they nevertheless must be the result and the fruit of our salvation. James sums up the matter in that much-misunderstood verse:

> Ye see then how that by works a man is justified, and not by faith only (James 2:24).

Now on the surface this does seem like a flat contradiction of Paul's statement, "Therefore by the deeds of the law there shall no flesh be justified in his sight: for by the law is the knowledge of sin" (Romans 3:20). How can we reconcile the teaching of Paul's "justification by grace without works" and the teaching of James' "justification by works." Do they contradict each other? To understand this scripture as well as any other, we must always ask two questions. First, to whom is he talking? and second, what is he talking about? Apply this rule to the teaching of Paul and James. Paul in Romans is telling us how a sinner can be justified in God's sight, and that is by faith alone. The key phrase is, "in his (God's) sight." How can a sinner be saved and justified in God's sight? The answer is: by faith, and faith alone. But James is discussing the question, How can this believer, already justified in the sight of God, now be justified in the sight of men? The answer is: by works. God sees faith in the heart of the repentant sinner, and declares him justified, but men will never know it, until they see it in the conduct and works of this saved man. We are justified in God's sight by faith; we are justified in the sight of men only by our works. Faith is the *root*, and works are the *fruit*.

Both Paul and James refer us to the life of Abraham as an example of justification by faith, and by works. Paul calls our attention to an entirely different incident in Abraham's life than does James. Abraham was justified in the sight of God when he believed what God said concerning a promised son. Romans 4:3 says,

> . . . Abraham believed God, and it was counted unto him for righteousness.

It was faith without works. But when James uses Abraham as an example of justification by works, he refers us to an experience in Abraham's life which was many years after. It was his sacrifice of his son Isaac in obedience to God. This was the public demonstration of his faith. By this act of supreme sacrifice he *proved to men* the reality of his faith in God. James therefore says:

> Was not Abraham our father justified by works, *when he had* offered Isaac his son upon the altar? (James 2:21).

Note these words, *when he had* offered his son. Abraham had been justified by faith in God's sight over thirty years previously, but now when (after) he had offered up his son, he justified his faith in the sight of all men. This is the answer to the error of antinomianism, which teaches that since we are saved by grace, it makes no difference how we live. It is an error just as serious as legalism.

There was a third error in the days of Paul concerning the ministry of the law. In addition to the error of legalism and antinomianism, there is another called in theological language, *Galatianism*, because it was most prevalent in the churches in Galatia. It teaches that we are saved by grace without works, but then after we are saved we must be *kept* by perfect obedience to the law. In simple language, it is "saved by faith and kept by works"; or "saved by grace and kept by keeping the law." This is a subtle deception of the enemy of our souls, for, having once been delivered from the law, it would put us back again under its legal bondage for our ultimate and final salvation. It is a flat denial of salvation by grace, for in the end our salvation becomes dependent upon *our* behavior and the works of the law.

To refute this evil error of "saved by grace—kept by works," the Holy Spirit inspired the Apostle Paul to write one whole epistle to show the terrible mistake of making salvation partly dependent on our behavior. It is the epistle to the Galatians. The Galatians had believed Paul's teaching of salvation *by grace*. But then false teachers had come in who said, "Oh, no, Paul was mistaken; it is true that we are saved by simple faith without works, but after that, you are on your own. Whether or not you will finally arrive, now depends on *you* and your perfect obedience to the law." Listen to Paul's stinging answer in Galatians 3:

> O foolish Galatians, who hath bewitched you, that ye should not obey the truth, . . .
> Are ye so foolish? having begun in the Spirit, are ye now made perfect by the flesh? (Galatians 3:1, 3).

"What!" asks Paul, "Do you think that God would save you by His grace, and then make the future possession of this gift dependent upon *us*?" And to clinch the folly of trying to hold on, and keep from losing our salvation, he says:

> For as many as are of the works of the law are under the curse: for it is written, Cursed is *every one* that *continueth not* in *all things* which are written in the book of the law to do them (Galatians 3:10).

Those of you who imagine that you can hold on to your salvation by your own behavior in keeping God's law, will you read that verse slowly and carefully, emphasizing these words: *cursed, every one, continueth, all things*. I too would ask you the question which Paul asks, "Are you so foolish, having begun in the Spirit (by grace), are you now made perfect (kept to the end) by the works of the law?"

The Truth of Grace

Having seen the three errors which have plagued the church since the days of the apostles, we turn to the glorious truth of our deliverance from the curse of the law, from beginning to end. Whenever we preach that we are kept, as well as saved by grace, we are accused of teaching a dangerous doctrine. We are accused of teaching license to sin. But that accusation is not a new one, for the apostle had to face the same criticism. After his statement, "Therefore we conclude that a man is justified by faith without the deeds of the law" (Romans 3:28), he anticipates an objection, and says:

> Do we then make void the law through faith? God forbid: yea, we establish the law (Romans 3:31).

When we state that no man can keep the law of God perfectly, do we by that statement downgrade the law? Do we make void the law? Do we by this assertion weaken the law or accuse it of imperfection? Is this belittling the law, when we say it is so high, so holy, and perfect, that no man can attain unto it by himself? God forbid, says Paul. The very opposite is true—"We establish the law." We prove its perfection, its holiness, its high standard, by exalting it far above the attainment of sinful man. Because the law is holy, sinful man cannot keep it. Because it is perfect, no imperfect mortal can satisfy its perfect require-

54   *Law or Grace*

ments. Because it is just, it must condemn and punish the unjust sinner. "Yea," says Paul, "we establish the law." We prove its perfection.

KEPT BY HIS GRACE

Paul knew better than to claim salvation by his own efforts. He rested completely in the grace of God, not only to save him, but to keep him as well. He said,

> . . . I know whom I have believed, and am persuaded that he is able to keep that which I have committed unto him against that day (II Timothy 1:12).

And again,

> Being confident of this very thing, that he which hath begun a good work in you will perform it until the day of Jesus Christ (Philippians 1:6).

No, says Paul, it is all of grace, from beginning to end, or it is not grace at all. Before we close this message we must answer a question which is sure to be raised. Are we then without duty or obligation to keep God's law? Ah, no! The law still stands to condemn sin, and the sinner. But the believer, delivered from the judgment and penalty of the law, now is living under a *new law*; namely, the law of liberty and of love. To be sure, the believer desires to keep God's law, but his motive is entirely changed. He does not strive to keep God's law in order to earn his salvation or to escape judgment, but now he seeks to keep that law and to please God, because of gratitude to God for His deliverance from the curse of that law. The law of love now takes the place of the law of sin and of death.

Here is an illustration. I have before me on my desk a needle. It lies quietly on the glass, held down by the law of gravity, a pull from below—the attraction of the earth beneath. As long as this law alone operates it will hold that needle down. But it can be overcome by another law. I now take a magnet, hold it above that needle, and I overcome the law of gravity by a more powerful force, the pull of magnetism from above. I did not abolish the law of gravity, or suspend it, but it is overcome by the law from above. The gravity, the pull from beneath, is not diminished; it is still as powerful as ever. So, too, when we are saved, we do not dishonor the law by saying we are not under its power any more, but we are now under the higher law of love. The believer now seeks to please God, because of His love and not because of fear of condemnation. One verse should clinch the matter for all:

> For this, Thou shalt not commit adultery, Thou shalt not kill, Thou shalt not steal, Thou shalt not bear false witness, Thou shalt not covet; and if there be any other command-ment, it is briefly comprehended in this saying, namely, Thou shalt love thy neighbor as thyself.
>
> Love worketh no ill to his neighbor: therefore *love is the fulfilling of the law* (Romans 13:9, 10).

If we love God we will seek to obey Him. If we love our neighbor, we will not seek to harm him. The more love, the less law; and the less love, the more the law is needed. Why do you seek to obey God and keep His commandments? Is it because of fear of punishment, fear of chastening, fear of losing your salvation? Or is it because "perfect love casteth out fear" and now your motive is gratitude and love for such a great salvation? Ask yourself the question today, Why do I seek to live a life pleasing to God? Is it fear, or is it *love?*

Chapter Seven

THE LIMITATIONS OF THE LAW

> For the law was given by Moses, but grace and truth
> came by Jesus Christ (John 1:17).

For over twenty-five hundred years man lived without a
written law. The Ten Commandments written on tables of stone
were given by God through Moses to the children of Israel at
Mount Sinai. Adam, Noah, Abraham, Isaac, and Jacob knew
nothing of these commandments written on tables of stone. They
were under another law, the law of conscience. As soon as man
sinned and Adam fell, he became aware of this law of conscience.
The tree of the knowledge of good and evil may very well be
called the tree of *conscience*. Before he fell, man knew no evil,
but as soon as he sinned he was accused by a conscience which
he did not possess before this. Satan had promised this, for in
the temptation he had said:

> For God doth know that in the day ye eat thereof [the
> tree of the knowledge of good and evil], then your eyes shall
> be opened, and ye shall be as gods, knowing good and
> evil (Genesis 3:5).

Immediately, therefore, after the fall, man acquired a consciousness of guilt, as evidenced by his frantic effort to hide his
nakedness and to avoid meeting God. He as yet knew nothing
of the law or the Ten Commandments, but he did have within
him a voice which told him some things were inherently, morally
wrong. This was the law of conscience. This consciousness of
guilt, this sense of right and wrong, is the universal possession of
all men. There is not a people or tribe on the face of the earth,
no matter how uncivilized, which does not know that it is wrong
to steal, wrong to kill, wrong to lie, wrong to commit adultery.
Conscience alone teaches man that these things are wrong,
without a written law. Listen to Paul as he says:

> For when the *Gentiles*, which have *not* the law, do by
> nature the things contained in the law, these, having not the
> law, are a law unto themselves (Romans 2:14).

What is this law? It is the law of conscience which condemns
them, for Paul adds, after saying that the Gentiles *without* the
law are a law unto themselves,

> Which [that is the Gentiles who know nothing of the law]
> shew the work of the law [that is, condemnation] written
> in their hearts, *their conscience also bearing witness,* and
> their thoughts the mean while accusing or else excusing one
> another (Romans 2:15).

Paul does not say that the Gentiles have God's law written in
their hearts, but the *work* of the law, which is condemnation.
Conscience condemns man, and by his conscience he shall be
judged. Now man was under this law of conscience for 2500
years before God gave His written law on Sinai. Paul tells us the
law was *four hundred and thirty years after* God's covenant to
Abraham (Galatians 3:17).

This law of conscience, however, was an unreliable guide for
man, for it only convicted him of things committed against his
fellow man, such as stealing, lying, murder, etc., as later embodied in the second table of the law. But conscience could not
teach man anything about his duty toward God. He had no conscience concerning the first four commandments embodied in
the first table of the law. That called for a supernatural revelation. How did man know it was wrong to serve other gods,
when he had received no law against it, and did not know the
true God? How could man know it was wrong to worship idols
when it had never been prohibited? How did the Gentiles who
did not have the Word of God know it was sin to use the name
of God in vain? They didn't even know the name of the true
God! How did they know anything about sabbath-breaking
when the sabbath law was utterly unknown to them, and was
not given until upon Mount Sinai? All these things conscience
could not reveal to man.

CONSCIENCE FLEXIBLE

Moreover, conscience is not a reliable guide, for conscience
varies in different individuals. Conscience permits some people

to do some things, which are considered evil and wicked by others. Then, too, conscience may be dulled, seared, or may become weak or imperfect. Now the Lord permitted the Gentiles to live under this law of conscience, and they will be judged by this law. They will be held accountable for what they did know, not by what they did *not* know. Under conscience there could, of course, be no improvement, and so when Israel left Egypt, He gave them a new revelation contained in the law of commandments, laws, ordinances, and precepts, to reveal how far short man under conscience had come, and to reveal the awfulness and exceeding sinfulness of sin. This then was the beginning of the law, when it had been proven that the elastic, flexible conscience of man could never show him his real condition before God. To the question, therefore, of Paul in Galatians 3:19, we notice that the law was dispensational in character. Paul had asked the question, "Wherefore then serveth the law?" (Galatians 3:19).

The Bible gives a number of reasons, which we wish to take up in some detail. We may classify the answer as follows: the law was *dispensational* in character; *national* in its demands; *exemplary* in its purpose; *demonstrational* in its application; and *final* in its condemnation. We take up each one in some detail. The question was, "Wherefore then serveth the law?" It is an important question, for if the law cannot save, cannot justify, cannot sanctify, cannot keep us, then what good is it anyway? It was first of all *dispensational* in character. There were 2500 years when man was without this law. It was given to Moses on Mount Sinai, and was fulfilled on Calvary. And today we live in the dispensation of the grace of God.

IT WAS NATIONAL

Secondly, the law was *national*; that is, it was given to one definite, particular nation, the nation of Israel. Now do not misunderstand. We did not say the law was not *for* us, but it was not given *to* us. To be sure, the law contains the eternal statement of the will of God. It is God's declaration to all the world, laying down the requirements of a holy God. It is the perfect expression of God's holiness, eternally true. But the law was given to the nation of Israel as an example, as we shall see later on. To indicate the national character of the law, notice how the law opens:

> And God spake all these words, saying,
> I am the LORD thy God, which have brought thee out of the land of Egypt, out of the house of bondage (Exodus 20:1, 2).

It is addressed to the nation of Israel. We may make the application to ourselves as typified by Egypt and the house of bondage. That is a legitimate application, but by primary interpretation the law was given to the nation of Israel. The reason for this we shall discuss later. This national character of the law is clear from the passage we referred to previously:

> For when the Gentiles, which have *not* the law . . . (Romans 2:14).

In describing the Gentile nations who had violated the law of conscience, Paul says:

> Now we know that what things soever the law saith, it saith to them who are under the law: that every mouth may be stopped, and all the world may become guilty before God (Romans 3:19).

EXEMPLARY

This verse tells us the law was given to Israel as an example to the whole world. It was tried out, as it were, on one nation, in order to stop every mouth which would claim that the law could bring salvation. Paul says the law was given to Israel as a test, in order that the whole world, including Israel, might be found guilty before God. God tested one nation with advantages which no other nation ever enjoyed, and the failure of this one nation makes it unnecessary to try it on any less-favored people. There is no further proof needed. For over 1500 years Israel lived under this law, under the most salutary conditions, and yet at the end of fifteen centuries not one single Israelite had been saved by the law. The experience of Israel (for to them alone this law was revealed) proved that the law could not change the human heart. We ask the question, "What was wrong with that law that it failed to save a single individual?" The answer is *nothing*. Nothing was wrong with the law. It was the human heart which was wrong. By the experience of Israel, God proved to man that salvation could not be by the law. It proved its perfection when imperfect men could not keep it. If the nation of Israel was unable to keep that law of God, then it follows that no one else can, for God gave this nation every advantage: a separated homeland, a relevation of Himself, a holy priesthood, godly prophets; and yet—and yet, with all these advantages, they failed.

An Example

To illustrate the giving of the law to Israel in order to prove to the whole world that it could not save anyone, imagine a farmer from Central America moving to northern Canada. He rents a 640-acre farm and tells the owner of the farm he plans to raise bananas. However, the landlord objects and tells him that it cannot be done. Neither the soil nor the climate is adapted to producing bananas. But the man insists, saying he has had years of experience raising bananas in the tropics, while the Canadian farmer says he has had years of experience farming in Canada and *knows* it cannot be done. But the banana man insists, and so to prove its impossibility and to convince the tenant of his folly, the owner gives his consent. He decides to set aside just one acre of the best-suited ground of the entire farm. No use planting the whole 640 acres in bananas unless it is first tested and proven on the most likely place. A spot is chosen in the lee of the mountain, with south exposure. Here the soil is the best and the temperature the highest. The ground is thoroughly worked, liberally fertilized, and the best of plants are procured, and all summer the best of care in cultivating the plants is given. But in August there is a frost and the crop fails. No bananas!

Not discouraged, the man tries it again the next year, for after all, you can't judge by one season. The second year it is the same early frost, and then the third year the frost comes in July. They try it another year—same result. No bananas! And then another and another. Now suppose they try it for fifteen hundred years, and yet no bananas. Finally the boss says, "Now are you convinced you cannot raise bananas on this farm in Canada?" But the man says, "Let's try it out on the rest of the farm." This would be folly, for if it cannot be done on the most likely and advantageous spot, it certainly cannot succeed under less favorable circumstances.

ISRAEL—GOD'S GARDEN

This illustration should make clear the statement of Paul in Romans 3:19, 20,

> Now we know that what things soever the law saith, it saith to them who are under the law [Israel]: that *every mouth may be stopped,* and *all the world* may become guilty before God.
> Therefore by the deeds of the law there shall no flesh be justified in his sight: for by the law is the knowledge of sin (Romans 3:19, 20).

Israel's experience was to show the impossibility of salvation by the law—*no bananas.* The law was given to Israel to stop the mouths of all the world who would teach salvation by the law. God gave the law to the most favored nation in the world. Israel imagined she could keep God's law. So God gave them a law, a perfect, holy, and just law. Then He planted Israel in the promised, sheltered land of Canaan. He drove out their enemies for them. He gave them a ritual and the oracles and ordinances. He gave them priests, and godly prophets to teach them. Under the most promising and helpful circumstances He gave them a perfect law to keep, and after 1500 years it was a complete failure—*no bananas.* Does God have to test it out on the rest of the world? Does He have to permit you to try it? No, no, my friend! Every mouth has been stopped. The whole world is proven guilty before God.

When Israel had proven that the law could not save, for it was not intended to do so, God sent His Son into the world to *keep the law and pay its penalty,* suffer its condemnation, and curse, and now offers salvation full and free through grace by faith in Him who,

> . . . hath redeemed us from the curse of the law, being made a curse for us . . . (Galatians 3:13).

Abandon all hope of saving yourself, and cast yourself on the mercy and grace of God, receive Christ, and He will impute to you, *not the condemnation* of the law, but its perfect righteousness.

But when the fulness of the time was come, God sent forth his Son, made of a woman, made under the law,

To redeem them that were under the law, that we might receive the adoption of sons (Galatians 4:4, 5).

Chapter Eight

THE ONE COMMANDMENT

For when we were in the flesh, the motions of sins, which were by the law, did work in our members to bring forth fruit unto death.

But now we are delivered from the law, that being dead wherein we were held; that we should serve in newness of spirit, and not in the oldness of the letter (Romans 7:5, 6).

When God gave the law to Israel He knew that not one single person would keep that law perfectly. He demanded obedience to that law, under penalty of death, knowing beforehand that they were unable to keep it. This does seem, on the surface, an unreasonable demand, unless we understand the purpose for which the law was given. It was not given to *save*, but to show the need of salvation. It was not given to take away sin, but to reveal sin, for by the law is the *knowledge* of sin (not salvation from sin). We therefore ask the question anticipated by Paul in Romans 7:7,

What shall we say then? Is the law sin? God forbid. Nay, I had not known sin, but by the law: for I had not known lust, except the law had said, Thou shalt not covet.

For I was alive without the law once: but when the commandment came, sin revived, and I died (Romans 7:7, 9).

The law did not produce sin, but instead it revealed the true nature of sin. Paul says, "when the commandment came," it slew me. What did Paul mean by *the* commandment? The two tables of the law are called the Ten Commandments. Which one of these did Paul refer to when he said, *the commandment?* I believe Paul indicates clearly to which one he referred. It is the last one—*thou shalt not covet.* He says,

. . . I had not known lust, except the law had said, Thou shalt not covet (Romans 7:7).

That was *the* commandment which caused sin to revive, "and I died," says Paul. Paul could claim perfect obedience to the first nine commandments as far as *outward* observance was concerned. He could say honestly,

> . . . If any other man thinketh that he hath whereof he might trust in the flesh [good works], I more:
>
> Circumcised the eighth day, of the stock of Israel, of the tribe of Benjamin, an Hebrew of the Hebrews; as touching the law, a Pharisee;
>
> Concerning zeal, persecuting the church; touching the righteousness which is in the law, blameless (Philippians 3:4-6).

Paul could claim outward observance to the law. He had kept every one of the commandments and said, "as touching the law, I am blameless." He could say he had never broken the first commandment—had never owned any other God. He could claim the second—he had never worshiped graven images. He could claim perfect obedience to the third—he had never taken the name of the Lord in vain; and so with the fourth—he had never broken the law of the sabbath. And so on, with the fifth, honoring father and mother; and the sixth, thou shalt not kill; and the seventh, adultery; and the eighth, stealing; and the ninth, bearing false witness, lying. To all these he could say, "I kept every one of them. No one can accuse me of not keeping those laws." But it applied only to outward observance, and now comes the tenth commandment, which Paul calls,

THE COMMANDMENT

It was a new view of sin, and revealed it as a matter of the heart and the mind, and not only the overt act itself. The commandment said, "Thou shalt not covet." Evil desire, covetousness, jealousy, wrong thoughts, sinful motives (even if never carried into action) are sin. *The* commandment now reveals that sin is not an *act*, but an attitude. It is a matter of the mind and heart, rather than of the body. Before the act of murder is committed, there is the sin of hate which prompted it. Before a person steals, there is first of all the sin of covetousness. Before the act of adultery is committed, there is the sin of lusting.

Jesus emphasized this aspect of sin when He said,

> For out of the heart proceed evil thoughts, murders, adulteries, fornications, thefts, false witness, blasphemies:

These are the things which defile a man . . . (Matthew 15:19, 20).

When Paul came face to face with *the* commandment, he had no more boasting of his outward observance of the law. Up to now Paul could say, I never cursed, broke the sabbath, worshiped idols, stole, or murdered anyone. He could say, as touching these things, I am blameless, but then *the commandment* came, and revealed to Paul the real nature of sin, that even evil desire is sin. This is the meaning of the verse,

> For I was alive without the law once: but when the commandment came, sin revived, and I died.
> And the commandment, which was ordained to life, I found to be unto death.
> For sin, taking occasion by the commandment, deceived me, and by it slew me.
> Wherefore the law is holy, and the commandment holy, and just, and good.
> Was then that which is good made death unto me? God forbid. But sin, that it might appear sin, working death in me by that which is good; that sin by the commandment might become exceeding sinful.
> For we know that the law is spiritual: but I am carnal, sold under sin (Romans 7:9-14).

THE LAW STIRRED UP SIN

We see then that the law brought to light the real nature of sin, not as an act but a *condition*, or an attitude. This is again expressed in Romans 7:5,

> For when we were in the flesh, the motions [movements] of sins, *which were by the law*, did work in our members to bring forth fruit unto death (Romans 7:5).

Notice carefully the words, "the motions of sins *which were by the law*." The motions of sins were caused by the law. The law was not sin, but it did set in motion the activities of sin. In verse 8, Paul says, "without the law sin was dead." The meaning is that sin was quiescent—it did not appear in its true light as sin. Then the law came and *stirred up sin*, so it became apparent and visible. The law did not cause or create sin, but it set it in motion —"drove it out of hiding," as it were. So in answer to the question, "Wherefore then serveth the law?" we add that it was:

REVELATIONAL

We have already seen that the law was national in character, dispensational in its ministry, and exemplary in purpose. We add now its *revelational character*. It revealed sin as it had not been seen before. Paul says, "the motions of sins which were by the law." Before the law, says Paul, sin was dead; that is, inactive and not visible. Sin was there, but it was made visible, "stirred up" by the law. An illustration may help. Imagine that I have on my desk a glass of water. It has stood there for a number of days, quiet and undisturbed. It has not been agitated, and we may call it "dead water." It looks clear and sparkling, but it is in reality badly polluted and unsafe to drink! It contains a large amount of impurities and particles of dirt. These filthy components are not visible to the eye, for they have all been deposited as a layer of sediment at the bottom of the glass. Because the water was dead, undisturbed, all the particles had gravitated to the bottom of the glass, quiet, undetected.

Now I take a teaspoon and begin to stir the water, and lo, immediately a film of milky, filthy material clouds the glass of water while a repulsive stench issues from the water. Now what have I done? I have stirred up something I did not know was there before. With the teaspoon I put in motion the pollution and impurities in the glass. Now notice carefully, the teaspoon did not corrupt the water or increase its pollution. Neither can the teaspoon purify the water. In order to do that, I remove the spoon and lay it aside. It was not intended to cleanse but to reveal. You see now what Paul means by the expression, "the motions of sins, which are by the law"—not the *sins* which were by the law, but the *motions of sins*. The spoon revealed the filth; but to purify the water, it must be distilled and the pure separated from the impure. This is not the ministry of the law, for by the law is the knowledge of sin.

THE SPOON IS THE LAW

The illustration of the water and the spoon is a picture of the human heart and the ministry of the law. The glass of water is the human heart. The law is the spoon which stirred up this sin within the heart. There is nothing wrong with the spoon, and there is nothing wrong with the law. The law cannot correct, or remove sin from the heart, just as the spoon cannot remove the impurities in the water. To purify the water takes *distillation*; to correct the sin in the human heart requires *regeneration*. The law then, instead of correcting the pollution, stirs it up.

The depravity of the human heart has done strange things to man. It has twisted and perverted his nature so that a forbidden thing seems more appealing than the things which are not prohibited. If you put up a sign on a fence, *Do Not Touch—Wet Paint*, it is a sure thing that someone will want to touch it to see if it is really wet. A sign, *Keep Off the Grass*, is an invitation to walk on it, so we have to build a little fence around it, in addition to the sign. Prohibitions are invitations to the sinful heart of man, to do the things they would not even think of doing, if they were not forbidden.

If you want to test out this propensity of the human heart, you can try it out in a very simple way. Suppose on the top shelf of your cupboard are several pots and pans. They have been there for quite a while and have never created a desire in the heart of, let us say, your six-year-old son. But now you say to him, "Jimmy, do you see that gray pot, the one next to the end one, on the right? Well, I don't ever want you to look inside it. You are not to touch it or try to find out why you are forbidden to do so." Now what have you done? You have created in the heart of that child a desire for something he never knew before, an insatiable desire to look into that jar and find out why mother doesn't want him to know what is in it. Just as sure as he is a chip off the old block, he will await his opportunity, and when he feels he is safe from detection, he will climb up and find out. Now as a mother, you have a right to forbid him to look into the jar or bowl, in order to teach him to know something about his own heart. This is the meaning of Paul's words, "for the motions of sins, which were by the law, did work in our members to bring forth fruit unto death" (Romans 7:5). And then notice the question of Paul,

> What shall we say then? Is the law sin? God forbid . . .
> (Romans 7:7).

There was nothing wrong with your demand for obedience concerning the bowl or the cookie jar. No, there was nothing wrong with the law—there was nothing wrong with the teaspoon. It was sterling silver. But the teaspoon did bring to light the impurities of the water, and so too, the law "stirred up the sin" which was not evident until the commandment came.

What the Law Could Not Do

In this connection let us refer again to the statement that the law was never designed to give life. It was a ministry of condemnation for the transgressor. Before we close this discussion, notice carefully Paul's statement in Galatians 3. After asking the question in verse 19, "Wherefore then serveth the law?" and the answer which we are discussing, he says:

> Is the law then against the promises of God? God forbid: for if there had been a law given which could have given life, verily righteousness should have been by the law.
> But the scripture hath concluded all under sin, that the promise by faith of Jesus Christ might be given to them that believe (Galatians 3:21, 22).

Could anything be clearer than this? If it were possible to give a law that could justify a sinner, then Christ would not have needed to die, but now salvation is free to all who turn away from the law as their hope of salvation, to faith in Jesus Christ.

> For what the law could not do, in that it was weak through the flesh, God sending his own Son in the likeness of sinful flesh, and for sin, condemned sin in the flesh:
> That the righteousness of the law might be fulfilled *in us* [not *by us*], who walk not after the flesh, but after the Spirit (Romans 8:3, 4).

Trust Him Today!

Chapter Nine

THE RIGHTEOUSNESS OF THE LAW

If the believer is delivered from the law (Romans 7:6); dead
to the law (Galatians 2:19); free from the law (Romans 8:2);
and redeemed from the law (Galatians 3:13; 4:5; and 5:18);
and Christ is the end of the law (Romans 10:4); does this mean
he can do as he pleases, break the law and live like the Devil,
and still go to Heaven unpunished? This is a perennial question
which is repeatedly raised by those who do not understand
either the nature, purpose or the ministry of the law. We receive
hundreds of letters from listeners who accuse us of preaching
license to sin, and being antinomian. To these we reply that
the Apostle Paul was accused of this same thing nineteen hundred years ago. Paul preached that the believer is not under the
law, and he was persecuted for it. Listen to Paul's enemies. They
said Paul taught that since we were not under law, sin was
permitted and even encouraged in order that grace might the
more abound. Listen to Paul's own words:

> For if the truth of God hath more abounded *through my
> lie* unto his glory; why yet am I also judged as a sinner?
> And not rather, (as we be slanderously reported, and as
> some affirm that we say,) Let us do evil, that good may
> come? whose damnation is just (Romans 3:7, 8).

Note well the accusation against Paul. They accused him of
teaching to do evil, that it might be overlooked by God, in order
to demonstrate God's goodness, by winking at sin and giving
license to sin. Paul calls these critics, *slanderers*. He says, "That
is slander!" And I can echo the words of Paul and tell anyone
who affirms that I teach that grace, security and freedom from
the law give license to sin, is a slanderer; and then Paul adds,
"whose damnation is just." No one! No one who understands
the claims of grace ever teaches that grace permits sin. Paul
emphatically denies the charge. Listen to him once again:

69

> What shall we say then? Shall we continue in sin, that
> grace may abound?
> God forbid. How shall we that are dead to sin, live any
> longer therein? (Romans 6:1, 2).

In this connection we call your attention to a clinching passage by Paul. In writing to Timothy he mentions the legalists
who had slanderously accused him of teaching freedom from the
law as an excuse for sin. Listen to what Paul says about them:

> Now the end of the commandment is charity [love] out of
> a pure heart, and of a good conscience, and of faith un-
> feigned:
> From which some having swerved have turned aside unto
> vain jangling [apparently about the law];
> Desiring to be teachers of the law; understanding neither
> what they say, nor whereof they affirm (I Timothy 1:5-7).

PAUL'S APPRAISAL OF LEGALISM

Notice Paul's appraisal of the legalists who do not understand
that *love* is the fulfilling of the law, springing from a purified
heart and unfeigned faith. This, Paul says, my critics who slander
me don't understand. It is well to repeat Paul's appraisal of them.
He accuses them of vain jangling about the law,

> Desiring to be teachers of the law; understanding neither
> what they say, nor whereof they affirm (I Timothy 1:7).

Then follows Paul's answer. Paul does not downgrade the
law, or deny its perfection and holiness and justice. He says,

> But we know that the law is good, if a man use it lawfully
> (I Timothy 1:8).

Ah, yes! There is nothing wrong with the law, but the trouble
is with those who try to keep it. And now follow closely Paul's
argument. Before we read it, remember we said the *believer is
not under the law*. To whom then does it apply? Pay close
attention to I Timothy 1:9-11,

> Knowing this, that the law is not made for a righteous
> man, but for the lawless and disobedient, for the ungodly and
> for sinners, for unholy and profane, for murderers of fathers
> and murderers of mothers, for manslayers.
> For whoremongers, for them that defile themselves with

mankind, for menstealers, for liars, for perjured persons, and if there be any other thing that is contrary to sound doctrine;

According to the glorious gospel of the blessed God, which was committed to my trust (I Timothy 1:9-11).

NOT FOR THE RIGHTEOUS

Note carefully the opening words of this passage, "knowing that the law is not made for a righteous man." A righteous man who has never broken the law in any manner at any time has nothing to fear from the law. It has no claim upon him if he is not guilty. The law does not punish the innocent or the righteous. It only punishes transgressors. If there had ever lived a man who kept God's law perfectly, he would be totally free from any obligation or fear of punishment. But such a man never lived, for David said:

> The LORD looked down from heaven . . . , to see if there were any [one] that did understand, and seek God (Psalm 14:2).

And what did God find? Did He find any *righteous men?* *Listen,*

> They are *all* gone aside, they are *all* together become filthy: there is *none* that doeth good, no, not one (Psalm 14:3).

And Paul under inspiration echoes the same verdict in Romans. He says it is a proven fact that *all* men are under sin,

> As it is written, There is none righteous, no, not one:
> There is none that understandeth, there is none that seeketh after God.
> They are all gone out of the way, . . . there is none that doeth good, no, not one (Romans 3:10-12).

The condemnation of the law is universal, without a single exception. Now let us go back to Paul's letter to Timothy:

> Knowing this, that the law is not made for a righteous man . . . (I Timothy 1:9).

But there is none righteous, so who is it then for? The answer is devastating. It is for sinners, profane, murderers, whoremongers, thieves, liars, and the like. If you are guilty of any of these, you have reason to fear the law, for it condemns you. Those who say they are under the law, thereby admit (although they may not know it) that they are in the category of the sinners enumerated by Paul: lawless, disobedient, profane, filthy, murderers, whoremongers, and liars. The only way to escape the curse of the law upon these sins is to be a *righteous man—holy and sinless.*

WHO IS RIGHTEOUS?

We have seen that there is not a single Adam's son who is righteous. What a hopeless situation! But wait! While man does not possess a righteousness of his own, there is another who has provided a righteousness which can be imputed to the guilty sinner. This One who can provide the righteousness of the law is the Lord Jesus Christ, the only One who ever kept God's law *perfectly,* and then, in addition, paid the penalty of the broken law for unrighteous, guilty sinners. By His death on Calvary He atoned for the broken law; by His resurrection He provided His righteousness to all who believe. And now see the result in those who believe. God accepts the payment of the penalty for sin which Jesus made when He died on the cross, and reckons it to the account of those who receive His offer of salvation by faith. The penalty for sin is paid, and there is no condemnation. And then that pardoned sinner is clothed in the sinless righteousness of the Lord Jesus Christ, and stands in God's sight, as though he had never sinned, but is as holy *in Christ* as the law demanded. The sinner has by imputation of Jesus' righteousness become a justified saint. Ah, yes, he still is imperfect in his old nature, he still falls and fails in his walk, but in his position in the *sight of God* he is perfect and complete.

THE RIGHTEOUSNESS OF CHRIST

Such a justified sinner is called *righteous* before God because of the merits of the Lord Jesus Christ. God will judge him if he sins as a believer and fails to confess, but condemnation is forever past. Now go back to our Scripture in I Timothy:

> Knowing this, that the law is not made for a righteous man
> . . . (I Timothy 1:9).

The man or woman who has been declared *righteous* through God's grace by faith in Christ is therefore free from the condemnation of the law. But for all others, enumerated by Paul as sinners, murderers, liars, whoremongers (and this includes all who are not saved), the law continues to be God's requirement, and stands to condemn and damn everyone who is not in Christ. Listen again to Paul. Paul says he was once such,

> Who was before a blasphemer, and a persecutor, and injurious: but I obtained mercy, because I did it ignorantly in unbelief.
> And [but] the *grace of our Lord* was exceeding abundant with faith and love which is in Christ Jesus (I Timothy 1:13, 14).

Paul was under the condemnation of the law once, but then *grace* entered and he was set free. And so we ask again, What is the ministry of the law today, since Christ fulfilled its demands on Calvary? Its ministry is still the same in condemning the sinner who rejects Christ. While the believer is free from the law, delivered and redeemed, those who refuse the *righteousness* Jesus provided, are still under its threatenings. But to the believer it holds no threat any more, for he is *in God's sight, righteous.* How glorious the Word of God in Romans 3. After the sad news that "by the deeds of the law there shall no flesh be justified in his sight" (Romans 3:20), Paul continues with a

BUT!

> *But* now the righteousness of God without the law is manifested, . . .
> Even the righteousness of God which is by faith of Jesus Christ unto *all* and upon *all* them that believe . . . (Romans 3:21, 22).

What a glorious Gospel of grace. For all who reject God's righteousness, the law stands as the minister of judgment and *wrath*. Paul says,

> For the wrath of God is revealed from heaven against all ungodliness and *unrighteousness of men* (Romans 1:18).
> Because the law worketh *wrath* . . . (Romans 4:15).

In Colossians 3, Paul gives a list of sins which are condemned by the law, and says,

> For which things' sake the wrath of God cometh on the children of disobedience (Colossians 3:6).

But the believer is counted *righteous* in the sight of God. Abraham, the example of saving faith, "believed God, and it was counted unto him for righteousness" (Romans 4:3). Remember, the law was not made for a righteous man, and the only way you can be counted righteous in God's sight is by receiving the *righteousness* of the Lord Jesus Christ by faith. And then we pass under a higher law, the law of the Spirit of life which brings forth its fruit of righteousness.

But the fruit of the Spirit is love, joy, peace, longsuffering, gentleness, goodness, faith,

Meekness, temperance: *against such there is no law* (Galatians 5:22, 23).

And sinner, you may receive that righteousness, not by trying to keep the law, to make yourself worthy, but by coming empty-handed for mercy and grace.

But to him that worketh not, but *believeth* on him that justifieth the ungodly, his faith is counted for righteousness (Romans 4:5).

Chapter Ten

THE LAW AS A JUDGE

The last word of the Old Testament is "curse." *Curse!* This closes the book of the old covenant of the law to Israel. In this one word, "curse," the Holy Spirit sums up the ministry of the law—to condemn the sinner and teach him that he cannot be saved by the works of the law. But see the contrast in the way the New Testament closes. The dispensation of law ends in a curse—the dispensation of the grace of God through Jesus Christ ends as follows:

> The *grace* of our Lord Jesus Christ be with you all. Amen (Revelation 22:21).

How difficult it is for man to learn that the ministry of the law was to curse the transgressor, and could only bless those who kept its precepts perfectly and continuously. Since there has never been an Adam's son who was able to keep God's law perfectly, so the law could not bless anyone but only curse all,

> For all have sinned, and come short of the glory of God (Romans 3:23).

Some of the difficulty arises from the fact that so many believe that every time the word "law" appears in the Bible it refers to the Ten Commandments. This results in utter confusion. In only a bare minimum of instances does the term "law" refer exclusively to the Ten Commandments. In the great majority of cases it refers to the *Word* of God, or parts of that Word. We give as an example, Psalm 19 which is an exaltation of the Word of God. David uses many different terms to describe this Word, including the word "law." Notice verses 7 to 9:

> The *law* of the LORD is perfect, converting the soul: the *testimony* of the LORD is sure, making wise the simple.
> The *statutes* of the LORD are right, rejoicing the heart: the *commandment* of the LORD is pure, enlightening the eyes.

The *fear* of the LORD is clean, enduring for ever: the *judg-ments* of the LORD are true and righteous altogether (Psalm 19:7-9).

In these verses as in the whole Psalm, David is extolling the *Word* of God, and not only the Ten Commandments. Notice he calls the Word of God:

1. The *law* of the Lord.
2. The *testimony* of the Lord.
3. The *statutes* of the Lord.
4. The *commandment* of the Lord.
5. The *fear* of the Lord.
6. The *judgments* of the Lord.

All these are different names for the Word of God and have no specific reference to the Ten Commandments. In the vast majority of cases where the word "law" is used, it refers to the Scriptures. Jesus Himself spoke of the books of Moses as "the law" as distinguished from the prophets (Matthew 7:12). The word "law" is used in the Bible more than 500 times (about 300 times in the Old Testament, and over 200 in the New). In most of these cases it has no specific reference to the tables of the Law. We mention this to emphasize the absolute necessity of determining what is meant by "the law," when we read it. We must determine whether it refers (1) to the Scriptures as a whole; or (2) to the five books of Moses; or (3) the whole body of ceremonial and civil and moral laws as given in Exodus and Leviticus; or (4) the tables of the law written by the finger of God. In every case a study of the context will determine which meaning is in view.

A CURTAIN OF SEPARATION

As an illustration we would refer you to a little-known passage of Scripture. It is found in the Second Corinthian epistle, chapter three. (May I urge, yea, press upon you the benefit of turning to it in your Bible, and have it open before you, as we study this important revelation. Have your Bible open, and check every statement I make, and you judge if it is the Scripture indeed). We begin in verse 2:

Ye are our epistle written in our hearts, known and read of all men:
Forasmuch as ye are manifestly declared to be the epistle

of Christ ministered by us, written not with ink, but with the
Spirit of the living God; not in tables of stone [the Ten Com-
mandments], but in fleshy tables of the heart.

And such trust have we through Christ to God-ward
(II Corinthians 3:2-4).

After this introduction Paul proceeds to give us an amazing
contrast between the *perfect* law of God, and His *perfect* grace.
He says,

Who also hath made us able ministers of the new testament [covenant]; not of the letter, but of the spirit: for the
letter killeth, but the spirit giveth life.

But if the ministration of death, written and engraven in
stones [the Ten Commandments] was glorious, so that the
children of Israel could not stedfastly behold the face of
Moses for the glory of his countenance; which glory was to
be done away (II Corinthians 3:6, 7).

Before we read further, notice that Paul is now speaking
about the *law* in its narrowest sense, as referring to the Ten
Commandments. Notice, he identifies what he means by "the
law." He is talking about the ministration of death, "written and
engraven in stones." The reference is unmistakable. He is speaking of the two tables of the law. He is contrasting this *law* with
grace. Remember, he is now talking about the Ten Commandments—the two tables of the *law*, and calls it:

1. The letter of the law, and then adds that,
2. The letter of the law killeth,
3. The law is a ministration of death, and
4. It was accompanied by glory, but this glory was to be done
away.

Again we remind you, Paul is talking about the Law, the
ministration of death, "written and engraven in stones"; i.e., the
two tables of the law. But there is more. Listen to the following
verses (II Corinthians 3:9, 11-16),

For if the ministration of condemnation [the Law] be
glory, much more does the ministration of righteousness
exceed in glory.

For if that which is done away [the glory of the Law] was
glorious, much more that which remaineth is glorious.

Seeing then that we have such hope, we use great plain-
ness of speech.

And not as Moses, which put a vail over his face, that the children of Israel could not stedfastly look to the end of that which is *abolished*:

But their minds [Israel's minds] were blinded: for until this day remaineth the same vail untaken away in the reading of the old testament; which vail is *done away* in Christ.

But even unto this day, when *Moses* is read [the Law], the vail is upon their heart.

Nevertheless when it shall turn to the Lord, the vail shall be taken away (II Corinthians 3:9, 11-16).

Here Paul adds to his description of the law. We have already seen that the law gave,

1. The letter—not the Spirit.
2. This letter killeth.
3. The law was a ministration of death.
4. It was accompanied by a temporary glory.

To these four Paul now adds:

5. The law was a ministration of condemnation (v. 9).
6. This condemnation was to be done away (v. 9).
7. It was to be abolished (v. 13).
8. The law was a veil that prevented approach to the presence of God (vv. 14-16).

This last ministry of the law as a separating *veil* gathers up the whole purpose and ministry of the law. It was a *veil*, a *curtain*, separating sinners from God. Sin and disobedience must be removed before God can accept the sinner. The law is so perfect that it must condemn the least infraction of its perfect standard. It demands the death of the transgressor and therefore stands as a barrier between the sinner and God. It is a veil, and that veil of blindness is upon everyone who seeks by his own works or by his own obedience to the law, to make himself acceptable to God. That veil must be taken away. This, of course, sinful man cannot do; it can only be done by One who is (1) sinless himself; and (2) able to pay for the sin of another. This was accomplished by Jesus when He bore our sins in His own *body* on the tree. Here He met the perfect demands of God's holy law, paid its penalty and removed the barrier and the veil for all who will receive him. To all others the veil remains, and the law continues to be for them "the ministration of death and condemnation."

THE RENT VEIL

This is the significance of the rent veil at Jesus' death, when "the veil of the temple was rent in twain from the top to the bottom" (Matthew 27:51). The barrier which prohibited man from entering into the holy presence of God is removed; and to those who now believe, free access is granted into the very presence of God, and we are invited to

> . . . come boldly unto the throne of grace, that we may obtain mercy, and find grace to help in time of need (Hebrews 4:16).

The law then can show us our danger, but it cannot lead us out. We remind you once more of the words of Paul in I Timothy:

> Knowing this, that the law is not made for a righteous man, but for the lawless and disobedient . . . (I Timothy 1:9).

The vital question is, Are you a *righteous* man or unrighteous? If you are righteous, the law has no dread for you. Since you have no righteousness of your own, you must turn to another, even "Jesus Christ the *righteous*" (I John 2:1).

Before we close this chapter, let us consider carefully the following contrasts between the perfect law of God, and the perfect grace of God:

1. The law prohibits us from coming to God—Grace invites us to come as we are.
2. The law condemns the sinner—Grace redeems him.
3. The law says, "*Do* this and live"—Grace says, "It is *done*."
4. The law says, "*Try*"—Grace says, "It is *finished*."
5. The law curses the sinner—Grace blesses the believer.
6. The law slays the sinner—Grace saves him.
7. The law shuts every mouth before God—Grace opens the mouth in praise to God.
8. The law condemns the best man—Grace saves the worst.
9. The law says, "Pay up what you owe"—Grace says, "It is paid."
10. The law says, "The wages of sin is death"—Grace says, "The gift of God is eternal life."
11. The law says, "The soul that sinneth, it shall die"—Grace says, "Believe and live."

12. The law reveals man's sin—Grace atones for his sin.
13. By the law is the knowledge of sin—Grace provides redemption from sin.
14. The law was given by Moses—Grace and truth came by Jesus Christ.
15. The law demands obedience—Grace gives power to obey.
16. The law was written on stone—Grace is written in the heart.
17. The law was done away in Christ—Grace abides forever.
18. The law puts us under bondage—Grace sets the soul at liberty.
19. The law genders fear—Grace brings peace and confidence.

We might add many more contrasts, but we would drive home these few, so that any who have imagined they can make themselves acceptable to God by their own works and righteousness, may turn from fleshly works to faith, and from self to Christ. My heart goes out to the many deluded souls who are so blind as not to see the liberty we have in Christ—not the liberty to sin, but liberty to *serve*.

I receive hundreds of letters from sincere souls who would try to convince me to go back under the law. Wastebaskets full of magazines, papers, articles, and letters reach my desk each week, trying to prove to me that I am still *under the law*. What a waste of time, paper, and postage. Do you think, my friend, that I would give up my position under the blessing of God's grace, and put myself back under the curse of the law? Do you think for one moment that I would give up my security in Christ, to go back to trying to keep myself saved by my own works? Do you think for one moment I would turn my back on Calvary, and go back to Sinai? or give up my salvation in Christ, for a life of miserable struggling to be saved or keep myself saved by my works? If I did, I would be denying the finished work of Christ, I would take credit for my salvation, instead of giving Him all the glory. *No! No! No!* and emphatically *no!* I do not frustrate the grace of God: for if righteousness come by the law, *then Christ is dead in vain* (Galatians 2:21). Perish the thought! With Paul I shall say,

> . . . I know whom I have believed, and am persuaded that *he is able* to keep that which I have committed unto him against that day (II Timothy 1:12).

Chapter Eleven

THE LAW AS A DEMANDING HUSBAND

Did you hear about the wife who married her second husband on the same day her first husband died? Well, there is the record of one woman who did just that, and surprisingly enough the account is found in your Bible. It is related by the Apostle Paul in Romans 7. Here is the interesting account. Read it carefully:

> Know ye not, brethren, (for I speak to them that know the law,) how that the law hath dominion over a man as long as he liveth?
> For the woman which hath an husband is bound by the law to her husband so long as he liveth; but if the husband be dead, she is loosed from the law of her husband.
> So then if, while her husband liveth, she be married to another man, she shall be called an adulteress: but if her husband be dead, she is free from that law; so that she is no adulteress, though she be married to another man (Romans 7:1-3).

There is nothing said in this passage about any interval between the death of the husband and her remarriage. Of course, we frown upon people who marry too soon after burying their first mate. We take it as a sign that she had little love or respect for him. But nowhere in the Bible is a time limit set. The moment the woman becomes a widow she is free from the law of her first husband and may legally be married to another. Custom and decency, however, have set a certain indefinite period of time which should elapse before remarriage.

AN ILLUSTRATION

However, this passage (Romans 7:1-3) is merely used as an illustration of another important truth. Paul has been speaking of the relationship of the believer to the *law* of God and the *grace* of God. The case of the remarried widow is only introduced to elucidate Paul's teaching on law and grace. It is not intended to be a doctrinal treatise on the evil of remarriage while the first mate is alive, although this truth is implied in the illustration. The illustration is true to God's Word, but its purpose is to set forth the great truth of the believer's *freedom from the law*. And so after giving the illustration, he proceeds immediately to the application, and says in verse 4:

> Wherefore, my brethren, *ye also* are become dead to the law by the body of Christ; that ye should be married to another, even to him who is *raised from the dead*, that we should bring forth fruit unto God (Romans 7:4).

Paul now compares the believer in Christ to a wife who became a widow by the death of her first husband, and then immediately was married to her second husband, on the very day her first husband died. In Paul's illustration, the first husband was the *law*, and her second husband was the Lord Jesus Christ. Right here we must remind you that this, by interpretation, applies first to the religious Israelite, a member of the nation who had been under the law for over 1500 years, but remained fruitless. But although by primary interpretation it applies to Israel, it is equally true of all, and serves as an example of the hopelessness of bringing forth spiritual fruit by the law. Let us now look more closely at these two husbands, the law and the Lord Jesus Christ.

The First Husband

Paul is of course addressing his fellow Jews in particular. This is evident from the opening verse:

> Know ye not, *brethren*, (for I speak to them that know the law,) . . . (Romans 7:1).

Paul had been preaching free grace to both Jew and Gentile alike, and then, as now, it stirred up a great deal of opposition among the Judaistic sabbatarian legalists of that day, who insisted that Gentile believers be placed under the law and become Jews (proselytes). Paul had furthermore been accused of preaching a message of license. He answers these legalists in the previous chapter (Romans 6) and says,

> For sin shall not have dominion over you: for ye are not under the law, but under grace (Romans 6:14).

To this declaration, "Ye are not under the law, but under grace," the legalists had strenuously objected; and Paul, anticipating the charge, continues:

> What then? shall we sin, because we are not under the law, but under grace? God forbid (Romans 6:15).

He then declares once more his freedom from the law, and concludes the chapter with the well-known and striking contrast of the ministry of law and grace:

> For the wages of sin is death; but the gift of God is eternal life through Jesus Christ our Lord (Romans 6:23).

Here law and grace are sharply contrasted. The penalty of the law for sin is death—the gift of grace is eternal life. It is only then that Paul introduces us to the widow of Romans 7. Husband number one, says Paul, is the law. Israel was married to this law at Sinai soon after their deliverance from the bondage of Egypt. We observe a number of things about this first husband, the law:

He was a hard and severe master. His demands were absolute, and the poor wife was unable to fulfill all its requirements. If she failed in one point, she was guilty of all. This husband, the law, demanded perfect, unbroken, complete obedience, and failing this, she came under condemnation. Try as she might, she could not please her husband, for remember that the law was not only holy, but it was *just*. But the wife was commanded to obey her husband, the law, even though she found it impossible to keep its requirements. As a result she was constantly under threat of punishment for disobedience. Unless deliverance comes, this poor wife must ultimately perish, for the penalty of the law was death. She must somehow be delivered from the judgment of her first husband, or die.

THE BARREN HUSBAND

One more thing is revealed about this "law husband." The union of this wife and the law remained childless; there was no fruit—no children. This was not the fault of the law, but of the wife. The wife is sterile and unable to bring forth the fruit of righteousness as long as she is dead spiritually. The law cannot produce the fruit of righteousness in the sinner. The law is powerful indeed—powerful enough to put to death the sinner, but it had no power to give life. The poor, weak wife must constantly sweat and labor and toil, only to be driven by greater threatenings of her exacting husband. What she really needs is *another husband.* She needs someone to deliver her from bondage. But she cannot have two husbands at the same time. This would make her an adulteress. Before she could be married to Christ, she must be free from her first husband—the law. But all its demands must first be met.

This brings us to the glorious truth of justification by faith. In the fullness of time Christ came, born of a woman, born under the law, to deliver them that were under the law (Galatians 4:4). He kept the law perfectly, then went to Calvary and paid the penalty for sin, removed the curse of the law with which her first husband had threatened her. Through faith we now become members of the Body of Christ, and God now reckons to the believer all that Jesus did in his behalf, and imputes to him the righteousness of Christ. Now the law cannot condemn us, for the price has been paid. The debt has been fully paid.

This then is the thrust of Paul's application of the illustration of the remarried widow;

> Wherefore, my brethren, ye also are become dead to the law by the body of Christ . . . (Romans 7:4).

The believer is dead to the law. The law has no power over a dead person. He is beyond its reach forever. The maximum penalty the law can impose on anyone is the *death* penalty. It can do no more. But the believer has died in Christ, and the law cannot touch him. Paul says,

> I am [have been] crucified with Christ . . . (Galatians 2:20).

And because he had been crucified, he could say:

> For I through the law am dead to the law, that I might live unto God (Galatians 2:19).

FRUIT UNTO GOD

One more thing we must mention about these two husbands, the law and Christ. While the first husband produced no children, the second husband is able to produce fruit in the heretofore sterile wife. Before we are saved, we are infected by the guilt of sin, we are defiled and spiritually diseased from birth, and therefore are spiritually sterile—childless. The disease of sin which caused the sterility must be cured and this is done by the second husband for all those who believe on Him. Notice how clearly our scripture states this:

> Wherefore, my brethren, ye also are become dead to the law by the body of Christ; that ye should be married to another, even to him who is raised from the dead, that *we should bring forth fruit unto God* (Romans 7:4).

Now the point of all this is as follows: while we are dead to the law by the body of Christ, yet we are not widows, for we are married to another, even Jesus our Lord. We have a new and better husband, and are under a higher law, the law of love. But, you may ask, Since the Christian is dead to the law and delivered from the law, has he then no longer an obligation to keep the perfect law of God? To be sure, he has, but it is from an entirely different motive. The believer now seeks to do God's will and keep His law, not from fear of punishment, but out of a heart of gratitude for his deliverance and his love for the Deliverer. The wife now lives to please her new husband (Christ) because she loves him, for he has delivered her from bondage. Under law it was coercion, for fear of punishment, under threat of judgment and death. Now the motive is love, gratitude, and a burning desire to serve him.

The Christian has a moral obligation to obey God in everything, but it is not just because the law demands it, or to escape punishment. God expects of us moral obedience to His will just as much and even more under grace, but He also gives us the willingness and power to do His will, and all motivated by *love* for our husband (Christ). I admit, if the first husband is dead, and the widow remains unmarried, she might become a dangerous character, but the case is not so at all. She is remarried to another, even Christ.

The power of *love* is infinitely greater than the power of law. It is for this reason *love* is the fulfilling of the law. Listen to Paul in Romans 13:10,

> Love worketh no ill to his neighbour: therefore love is the fulfilling of the law (Romans 13:10).

The more love, the less law is needed, and vice versa, the less love, the more law. Does a mother need a set of laws to tell her to care for her baby? For a servant or baby sitter we need rules, with instructions for feeding, caring, and protecting the child, but for the mother this would be an insult. She needs no commands to feed that baby, to keep it clean, to protect it, to keep it warm and comfortable, away from fire and danger. Her love makes all laws and commandments unnecessary. So, too, the Christian's service must be one of love for the Lord. If I love Him, I will not have any other gods, I will not worship heathen idols, I will not take His name in vain, or profane His holy day.

We can sum it all up by the following incident. A believer who was rejoicing in the liberty of grace and freedom from the law was asked, "Now, if you are not any more under law, then can you do anything you *want to*?" The Christian replied, "Yes, I can do whatever I want to, but when I was saved the Lord put a new *want to* in my heart." If it is not your desire to serve and please the Lord because you love Him, you need to re-examine your heart. God pity the poor Christian who walks the narrow road because he is afraid he will be punished or chastened if he does not behave. Yes, I pity the Christian who behaves himself because he is afraid he will be lost again if he wanders away. This is a mean, unworthy motive for service. The only service our Lord accepts is that which comes from a heart of gratitude and love.

We love him, because he first loved us (I John 4:19).

Chapter Twelve

THE LAW AS AN EXECUTIONER

> For I through the law am dead to the law, that I might live unto God.
>
> I am crucified with Christ: nevertheless I live; yet not I, but Christ liveth in me: and the life which I now live in the flesh I live by the faith of the Son of God, who loved me, and gave himself for me.
>
> I do not frustrate the grace of God: for if righteousness come by the law, then Christ is dead in vain (Galatians 2:19-21).

The Christian is a paradox, an apparent contradiction, for he is said to be both dead and alive; not half-dead or half-alive, but completely dead and completely alive. The true believer is dead to sin, and alive unto righteousness; dead to self and alive unto Christ; and as Paul states it, "dead to the law but alive unto God." This fact Paul declares without apology. He says:

> For I through the law am dead to the law, that I might live unto God (Galatians 2:19).

Dead to the law! What a startling, amazing statement, "dead to the law." Paul does not say the law is dead. Far be it from Paul to claim the law is dead. Full well he knew its power over him before his conversion. The law is very much alive today in cursing and condemning sin and threatening judgment to the transgressor. The law is still the ministry of wrath upon the sinner. All-conclusive are the words of Ephesians 5:6,

> Let no man deceive you with vain words: for because of these things [the sins mentioned in the previous verse] cometh the wrath of God upon the children of disobedience (Ephesians 5:6).

No, the law is not dead, but Paul says, "I am dead to the law." The law does not recognize me as even existing any more. It cannot touch me, for I am dead and the law cannot touch dead men. To understand what Paul meant by this startling statement, we must see the occasion in which it was said. In the verses preceding Paul's statement, he tells how Peter had come to Antioch and had entered fully into the fellowship of Gentile Christians, by eating with them, which was strictly forbidden by the law for a Jew. But when certain legalistic law teachers from Jerusalem came up, Peter withdrew himself from the Gentile Christians and placed himself back under the law. This so incensed Paul that he severely rebuked Peter for his double standard, and now he concludes with the statement, "For I through the law am dead to the law." As far as I am concerned, my relationship to the law is ended. Now just what is Paul saying? He says that in the eyes of the law I am dead, I am non-existent. An illustration will serve to show what Paul meant.

Imagine a man who has committed murder. According to the law, if found guilty he must be put to death. He is arrested, charged with murder, and brought to trial. The court is in session, and the judge is on the bench. The accused man hears the accusation and charge read to him. But before the trial is con-cluded, the accused man suffers a heart attack and drops dead in the courtroom. A doctor declares him dead, and signs his death certificate. Now what does the judge do? After the com-motion is over, does he call the court to order, and say, "Let us proceed with the trial of this dead man?" Of course not! You cannot try a dead man, or condemn him to death, for he is already dead. So the judge dismisses the case. It is closed forever, and he proceeds to the next case. In the case of the criminal in our illustration, he cheated the law, he circumvented the law. It was the prerogative of the law to execute the man, but he died before the law could put him to death.

Not So With Paul

But, says Paul, it was not thus in my case. I did not cheat or beat the law, but the law itself put me to death. Notice, therefore, three important words in our text:

I through the law am dead to the law.

Through or by the law I was put to death. The law itself found me guilty, and executed me. The law slew me. Again allow me to illustrate. Imagine again the criminal before the bar of justice. The witnesses are called and all testify to the guilt of the murderer. The judge declares him guilty and sets the day for sentencing. When that day comes, the judge reads from the law the penalty for murder. It is death for the criminal, and the judge orders the man to be hanged by the neck until he is dead, and sets the date for execution. The sentence is carried out, and on the appointed day the man is led to the gallows and hanged. The physician declares the man dead, and the case is closed. Now this man is not only dead to the law, but dead *through the law.* The law put him to death. It can do no more. The law is satisfied. This, says Paul, happened to me—"I through the law am dead to the law."

This is not the end of the story, however. Three days after this guilty man was executed, you meet this same man one early morning, walking down the street. At first you can't believe your eyes. You look more closely, but there is no doubt about it. The criminal is alive. You rush to the home of the judge, rouse him from his bed, and excitedly exclaim, "Judge, judge, remember the man who was executed three days ago? Well, he is alive! I saw him with my own eyes! Call the police, call the sheriff, call out the National Guard, and pick up this dangerous criminal! Hurry, judge!"

The judge is not impressed at all, and says, "Now just calm down, and we will look at the record." He takes down the record of the trial, the verdict of guilty, the account of the execution, the doctor's death certificate, and finally the words, "case closed." He looks at you and says, "That man is dead." But you say to him, "He is alive! I saw him!" "I'm sorry," says the judge, "according to the law this man died three days ago. According to the law the man is dead. He has paid the extreme penalty."

The man is legally dead, for the law cannot punish a man twice for the same crime. If the man is alive again, it is of no concern to the law. The law did not anticipate a resurrection. There is no provision in the law as to what to do in such a case. According to the law the man is dead, and since the law cannot punish twice for the same crime, he is free—dead to the law— through the law and in the eyes of the law. Now, says Paul, that is what happened to me. I was executed by the law, but was raised again.

WHERE? WHEN? HOW?

Paul, will you please tell us *when* this happened to you, *where* this took place, and *how* were you put to death? Paul has the answer ready. It is found in the next verse:

> I am [have been] crucified with Christ: nevertheless I live;
> yet not I, but Christ liveth in me . . . (Galatians 2:20).

You want to know where I died—it was at Calvary. When did I die?—when Christ died. How did I die?—by crucifixion. That is the meaning of Paul's words, "crucified with Christ." Now to understand this strange statement of Paul, we must turn to the Word of God concerning the members of the Body of Christ. When Christ hung on the cross, people saw only a physical, human body, nailed to a cross by hands and feet. But when God looked down upon Jesus on the cross, He saw *another body*, a spiritual body united to its head. God saw in Him the mystical body of believers, who are members of Christ and called His Body. God saw the head, Christ, and He saw the Body of Christ, consisting of individual members, which make up the Church, which is His Body. What happened to the Head of the Church that day on Calvary, God reckons as having happened to all His members, for the Church is a spiritual body.

> For by one Spirit are we baptized into one body . . . (I Corinthians 12:13).

God foreknew every one of His chosen ones from eternity as members of the Body of Christ,

> According as he hath chosen us in him [Christ] before the foundation of the world . . . (Ephesians 1:4).
> For we are members of his body, of his flesh, and of his bones (Ephesians 5:30).

As the body of Jesus hung upon the cross, God looked down from Heaven and saw the spiritual Body of Christ, the Church, hanging there *in Christ*. This is Paul's meaning when he says, "I was crucified with Christ." As a member of the Body of Christ in the mind of God I was nailed with Jesus to the Tree. But this was not all. When they took Jesus down from the Tree, they buried Him, the head with the body, and since we are members of His Body,

. . . we are buried with him by baptism into death . . .
(Romans 6:4).

But that is not all, for that same body arose. After three days
and nights, the tomb was found empty, not one member was
left behind. Since we are members of His Body, we too arose
with Him, and Paul says,

If [since] ye then be risen with Christ, seek those things
which are above . . . (Colossians 3:1).

But there is still more. Forty days later Jesus ascended into
Heaven, and took that Body along. In Christ, therefore, in the
mind of God every believer is already seated in Heaven. In our
physical bodies we are still here on earth, but positionally and
spiritually in Christ, we are already in Heaven. Listen to Paul's
testimony:

But God, who is rich in mercy, for his great love wherewith he loved us,
Even when we were dead in sins, hath quickened us [made
us alive again] together with Christ, (by grace ye are saved;)
And hath raised us up together, and made us sit together
in heavenly places in Christ Jesus (Ephesians 2:4-6).

Remember then that "we are members of the spiritual body
of Christ," and what happened to Him happened to every member of His Body. Yes, with Paul, every believer can say,

I am crucified with Christ: nevertheless I live . . . (Galatians 2:20).

The law has been satisfied by the Lord Jesus Christ, and,
therefore, as members of Him, God reckons it as though we
ourselves had paid the penalty. Yes, indeed, *dead to the law,
through the law!*

ARE WE THEN LAWLESS?

Before we close this chapter we must again answer the charge
of some who say this freedom from the law is a dangerous doctrine, and will result in looseness of living and practicing sin
without restraint. Anyone who makes this charge does not understand the grace of God. He has never understood the text:

For I through the law am dead to the law, *that I might live
unto God* (Galatians 2:19).

Free from the law—yes; but under law to Christ. Deliverance from the law gives liberty—not liberty to sin, but liberty to serve Christ without fear. We shall deal fully in our coming chapters with this false accusation that *grace* gives an excuse for careless living. It does just the opposite. Paul says:

> For the grace of God that bringeth salvation hath appeared to all men,
> *Teaching us* that, denying ungodliness and worldly lusts, we should live soberly, righteously, and godly, in this present world (Titus 2:11, 12).

The law demanded holiness—the grace of God produces it. If you are looking to the law to improve you, it is time you turned your eyes to the grace of God, and remember,

> For by grace are ye saved through faith; and that not of yourselves: it is the gift of God:
> Not of works, lest any man should boast (Ephesians 2:8, 9).

Chapter Thirteen

THE LAW AS A SCHOOLMASTER

Wherefore the law was our schoolmaster to bring us unto Christ, that we might be justified by faith.

But after that faith is come, we are no longer under a schoolmaster (Galatians 3:24, 25).

In our series of messages on *Four Pictures of the Law,* we come now to the last one—the law as a teacher or schoolmaster. It is given in answer to Paul's question in Galatians 3:19, "Wherefore then serveth the law?" or why was the law given anyway? If the law cannot save the sinner or keep the saint, then why did God give it anyway? If God knew that no one could or would keep the law perfectly, then what good was there in demanding obedience? We have seen in the past chapters some of the answers, and in this chapter we come to another reason for the giving of the law. Paul asks an anticipated question:

Is the law then against the promises of God? God forbid: for if there had been a law given which could have given life, verily righteousness should have been by the law.

But the scripture hath concluded all under sin, that the promise by faith of Jesus Christ might be given to them that believe.

But before faith came, we were kept under the law, shut up unto the faith which should afterwards be revealed (Galatians 3:21-23).

Once more Paul declares that the law was never given to save or make men righteous. We repeat it often because it is so often repeated in Scripture. It is stated once more in verse 21, which we quote again:

. . . for if there had been a law given which could have given life, verily righteousness should have been by the law (Galatians 3:21).

If it were possible for a person to attain righteousness by keeping the law, Paul is saying, it would have made the sacrifice of Christ unnecessary. Then to illustrate the ministry of the law he gives the picture of the ancient schoolmaster. He says, "the law was our schoolmaster to bring us unto Christ" (Galatians 3:24).

Before taking up the teaching of this figure, we must first give you the *key* to the proper interpretation. You will never understand what Paul is teaching here without the use of this *key*. The key is the distinction between two little pronouns, *we* and *ye*. They are used over and over again in this chapter. The little word *we* (and *our*) is used *four* times in verses 23 to 25. The little word *ye* (and *you*) is used *six* times in verses 26 to 29. In the next chapter (Galatians 4) the pronoun *we* occurs three times and the word *ye* occurs twelve times. The key to the understanding of Paul's teaching here is to take special note of whom, and to whom, he is speaking when he says *we* and *ye*. Wherever Paul in this chapter uses the pronoun *we*, he is speaking as a Jew to the Jews representing the nation of Israel under the law. When he uses the word *ye* he is speaking of the Christians—the Church, *under grace*. He distinguishes between *we* Jews and *ye* believers. Unless this distinction is recognized, only confusion results. Bearing this in mind, we now take up the Scripture. In verse 23 he says:

> But before faith came, *we* [Jews] were kept under the law, shut up unto the faith which should *afterwards* be revealed.
> Wherefore the law was *our* [the Jews'] schoolmaster to bring *us* [Jews] unto Christ, that *we* [Jews] might be justified by faith.
> But after that faith is come, *we* [Jews] are no longer under a schoolmaster (Galatians 3:23-25).

You see then that he is speaking of the nation of Israel (under the law) as "we." And then the pronoun changes as he addresses the believers under grace, consisting predominantly of Gentile believers, and he says to them:

> For *ye* [believers—the Church] are all the children of God by faith in Christ Jesus.
> There is neither Jew nor Greek, there is neither bond nor free, there is neither male nor female: for *ye* [believers—the Church] are all one in Christ Jesus (Galatians 3:26, 28).

ISRAEL AND THE CHURCH

Israel was under the law; the Church is under grace. Israel was under a schoolmaster, as is necessary for immature children; we are mature children of God placed as sons of God in the family of God. But someone objects, and says, "Does not the passage teach that the law is our schoolmaster and guide to bring us to Christ?" I remember years ago a godly minister friend of mine who took me to task for preaching freedom from the law, and said to me, "After all, we need the law to lead us to the Saviour." I replied that I had never read that in the Bible. He looked surprised and said, "I'll show it to you!" He pointed his finger at Galatians 3:24 and said, "There it is, read it. It says, 'The law is our schoolmaster to bring us to Christ.'" I looked at it, and replied, "I don't see it there. Where does it say that the law is our schoolmaster?" and almost angrily he said, "Can't you read? Right there it says, 'the law is our schoolmaster.'" I looked again, and said, "I am sorry, but it just doesn't say that at all. It says, 'the law *was*—not *is*—*was* our schoolmaster.' And it also says *our* (the Jews') schoolmaster."

What misunderstanding results from careless reading of the Word. There is a vast difference between *was* and *is*. So if you apply the key of *ye* and *we*, all becomes clear. He is writing as a member of the Jewish Nation, to the believers, the churches in Galatia, consisting predominantly of Gentiles, and says, "the law was *our* (writing as a member of the nation of Israel) schoolmaster"—not *your* schoolmaster.

UNTIL CHRIST

The word *schoolmaster* does not convey the real meaning of the word as used in the original. The Greek word is *paidagogos* or a child-trainer. It was a person who was held responsible for the disciplining and training of a child until he became "of age" in the family. The International Standard Bible Encyclopedia gives the best explanation I have been able to find. It says: "'Schoolmaster' is a translation of *paidagogos,* literally, 'child-leader.' This *paidagogos* was not a teacher but a slave, to whom in wealthy families the general oversight of a boy was committed. It was his duty to accompany his charge to and from school, never to lose sight of him in public, to prevent association with objectionable companions, to inculcate moral lessons at every opportunity, etc. He was a familiar figure in the streets, and the (sour) 'face of the *paidagogos*' and 'to follow one like a *paidagogos*' were proverbial expressions. Naturally, to the average boy the *paidagogos* must have represented the incorporation of everything objectionable. Hence St. Paul's figure may be paraphrased: 'The law was a *paidagogos*, necessary but irksome, to direct us until the time of Christ. Then was the time of our spiritual coming-of-age, so that the control of the *paidagogos* ceased.'" [1]

This excerpt from the encyclopedia is a most correct commentary on the meaning of Paul's words. The law was to Israel what this strict, rigid, exacting, disciplining trainer was to a growing boy. It watched him every minute, restraining, prohibiting, and threatening. However, when the boy became of age he was taken from under the *paidagogos* authority and accepted into the family with full liberty and privileges as a son of the father.

COMING OF AGE

This period of training, however, was only temporary, and ultimately ended. This Paul asserts in our scripture. The ministry of the law was only *until* Christ came. John said,

> For the law was given by Moses, but grace and truth came by Jesus Christ (John 1:17).

Paul teaches the same thing, and says:

> Wherefore the law *was* our schoolmaster to bring us unto Christ . . . (Galatians 3:24).

But the three words, *to bring us*, are in italics in Scripture, indicating that they are not in the original but were supplied by the translators. Untold confusion and misunderstanding has been caused by this oversight of the translators. Paul does not say that the law *is* our schoolmaster to bring us to Christ, but instead (omitting the italicized words) "the law *was our* (the Jews') schoolmaster *until* (or *up to*) Christ." This is made clear by the verse which follows (verse 25):

---

[1] *The International Standard Bible Encyclopedia*, (Grand Rapids; Eerdmans, 1960), Vol. IV, p. 2702. Used by permission.

But after that faith is come, we are no longer under a schoolmaster (Galatians 3:25).

Israel then was kept under the law until Christ should come, and then the law ceased to exercise its power and authority over those who believe. The true believer in Christ in this dispensation is not under the law as a *paidagogos* or taskmaster, but is a son of God under grace. The believer has graduated and is now ready to go to work. School is out for the Christian. The son now takes his place in his Father's business, and does joyfully and gladly and eagerly that which he was *commanded* to do under the law with its threatenings and penalties. After faith is come, says Paul, *we* (Jews) are no longer under the schoolmaster.

From We to Ye

And then he continues, now addressing the believers, members of His Body:

For ye are all the children of God by faith in Christ Jesus (Galatians 3:26).

Notice carefully the change of pronouns here from *we* to *ye*. The law was for the nation of Israel as a disciplinary preparation for the coming of Christ, but the believer on this side of the Cross (whether Jew or Gentile) is not under the schoolmaster, but "*ye* (believers) are all the children of God by faith." The believer today never was under the law as a schoolmaster, and so Paul adds:

There is neither Jew nor Greek, there is neither bond nor free, there is neither male nor female: for *ye* are all one in Christ Jesus.
And if ye be Christ's, then are ye Abraham's seed, and heirs according to the promise (Galatians 3:28, 29).

The promise was to Abraham by grace, long before the law was given on Mount Sinai. The law has done its perfect work. It has proven that salvation must be by grace and not by the works of the law. And today the believer is forever delivered from the penalty and curse of the law. But, until the sinner sees himself as having come short of God's demands, and flees to Christ for salvation, the wrath of God and the curse of the law still hang over him.

Israel before the coming of Christ had the law as a teacher and an exacting schoolmaster. The believer in this day of grace has as his teacher the Holy Spirit, and the Word of God in its completeness. God's grace teaches us that which the law was unable to do. The grace of God enables us to do by love, what all the threatenings of the law failed to do by commandments. It is at Calvary where we find atonement for our sins. Having graduated from the elementary school of the law, we now sit at the feet of our instructor, the Holy Spirit. The old teacher, the law, could show us where we were wrong, but could do nothing to correct it, could demand holiness but not provide it. Oh, sinner, cease your struggling to do what only Christ could do, and heed His call:

> Come unto me, all ye that labour and are heavy laden, and I will give you rest (Matthew 11:28).

Chapter Fourteen

WHAT THE LAW COULD NOT DO

The law of God is holy, eternal, perfect and good. It is the divine pattern of righteousness which God demands of those who would be saved by their own works, merits, and efforts. The law of God is powerful, demanding punishment for each transgression. It is absolutely just in treating all alike, and there is no respect of persons under the law of God. There are no exceptions, for "the soul that sinneth, it shall die." It is inflexible, and rigid, so that it makes no allowance for effort, no matter how sincere, if that effort fails to measure up to every single demand of the perfect law of God. The law condemns and curses every sinner. It knows no distinction between little sins and big sins as far as guilt is concerned. The demands of the law of God are absolute.

. . . Cursed is every one that continueth not in all things which are written in the book of the law to do them (Galatians 3:10).

It recognizes neither wealth nor influence nor position nor station, but says:

. . . there is no difference:
For all have sinned, and come short of the glory of God (Romans 3:22, 23).

The law of God is eternal and stands today as the pronouncer of wrath upon all who refuse to accept, by simple faith in the Lord Jesus Christ, God's means of deliverance from its power and condemnation and curse. We re-emphasize these assertions concerning the law, because we who preach grace and freedom from the law for *believers* in Christ are constantly accused of making void the law, as though it did not exist any more, or had no application to this Age of Grace. This is a false accusation, but it was already answered by the Apostle Paul nineteen hundred years ago. He too had been slandered and condemned for preaching liberty and deliverance from the law. We, therefore,

99

would answer our critics in the words of Paul himself in Galatians 2:21,

> I do not frustrate the grace of God: for if righteousness come by the law, then Christ is dead in vain.

Paul had been accused of making void the law. In Romans 3:31 he answers the critics:

> Do we then make void the law through faith? God forbid: yea, we establish the law (Romans 3:31).

Stop and think about these momentous verses for a moment. Paul says, "If man could obtain righteousness by keeping the law, then Christ has died for nothing." Consider carefully the implications. If any human being could possibly be saved by the law of God, then why did Jesus have to die for those who were able to save themselves? It certainly would be a tragic mistake if God should demand the death of His Son to save those who could save themselves without the sacrifice of Jesus. And this holds true even for the believer *after* he is saved. If the believer, once saved, were able to keep himself saved by the works of the law, then why do we need Him to intercede daily for us at the right hand of God? What a terrible accusation to bring against God, to say He wasted the work of Christ on the cross for those who were able by their own work to attain righteousness. If that is so, then "Christ is dead in vain." His death was wholly unnecessary and uncalled for.

We Establish the Law

Now notice the same truth as expressed in that other verse, (Romans 3:31,)

> Do we then make void the law through faith? God forbid: yea, we establish the law.

By confessing that the law cannot be kept by us, we are not debasing or downgrading the law or weakening it, but instead *we establish the law*. By our admission that we were unable to meet the demands of the law of God, we prove its perfection. We elevate it high above man's fallible efforts and works. To say that man can keep God's holy law, is to drag it down to our own imperfect level. I confess that God's holy law is so high, so good, so perfect, so holy, that I, a poor, weak, depraved sinner cannot in myself meet its high standards. I extol the holiness of the law and exalt it, and so establish its perfection by not lowering it to the depths of my imperfection. I establish the law by admitting that its standards cannot be attained by me, a depraved sinner, and that I therefore must turn to another for mercy, pardon, and forgiveness. It must ever be,

> Nothing in my hand I bring;
> Simply to Thy cross I cling;
> Not the labor of my hands
> Can fulfill Thy law's demands;
> Could my zeal no respite know,
> Could my tears forever flow,
> These for sin could not atone;
> Thou must save, and Thou alone.

This is Bible salvation. How conclusive the words of Paul:

> But to him that worketh *not*, but believeth on him that justifieth the ungodly, his *faith* is counted for righteousness (Romans 4:5).

WHAT THE LAW COULD NOT DO

We have seen that the law is powerful in *condemning* the sinner, but at the same time the law is also powerless to *save* that same sinner. It is also powerless to condemn the believer in Christ. The child of God is forever free from its condemnation. After Paul has given us a picture of the struggle between the two natures within him, he cries out for deliverance:

> O wretched man that I am! who shall deliver me from the body of this death? (Romans 7:24).

Paul does not claim sinless perfection even under grace. He is still conscious of the presence of his old nature, and admits his defeat. Listen to his testimony:

> For I know that in me [that is, in my flesh,] dwelleth no good thing: for to will is present with me; but how to perform that which is good I find not.
> For the good that I would I do not: but the evil which I would not, that I do (Romans 7:18, 19).

Now remember, this is Paul's testimony some twenty-five years after he had been saved. He still acknowledges the presence of his old nature and confesses his defeat. He continues to tell us of his earnest striving to please God, but how he fails in his own strength:

> I find then a law, that, when I would do good, evil is present with me.
> For I delight in the law of God after the inward man:
> But I see another law in my members, warring against the law of my mind, and bringing me into captivity to the law of sin which is in my members.
> O wretched man that I am! who shall deliver me . . . (Romans 7:21-24).

Notice Paul says, "I delight in the law of God after the inward man." This inward man is the new man, the new nature, the life of Christ which the believer received at conversion. This new nature delights in the law of God. It is the perfect desire of Paul to keep God's law perfectly. The new nature seeks to keep God's commandments. But alas! Paul says, I have to contend with another law—the law of sin and of death which is in my members. As much as Paul's inward man desired to measure up to the law's perfection, he found his old nature opposing him at every turn, or as he puts it:

> But I see another law in my members, warring against the law of my mind [the inward man], and bringing me into captivity to the law of sin which is in my members (Romans 7:23).

And then, recognizing the futility, the hopelessness of gaining victory in his own strength, and the utter defeat which results from his trying to keep God's perfect law by himself as long as the old nature is within him, he turns from his own efforts, and cries out:

> . . . who shall deliver me from the body of this death [the old nature]? (Romans 7:24).

And then he finds the answer. He must give up all confidence in his own efforts, and turn the whole matter over to another, and so he concludes:

> I thank God through Jesus Christ our Lord (Romans 7:25).

He is our victory; and even when we fail, it is *His* victory which is credited to our account. The chapter (Romans 7) closes with this confession:

> . . . So then with the mind [spirit] I myself serve the law of God; but with the flesh the law of sin (Romans 7:25).

This is the answer to the verse with which we began:

> For I know that in me (that is, in my flesh,) dwelleth no good thing . . . (Romans 7:18).

But, thank God, that is not the end of the story. The eighth chapter should follow the seventh without a break. After Paul admits his failure he cries out in Romans 8:1,

> There is therefore now no condemnation to them which are in Christ Jesus, who walk not after the flesh, but after the Spirit (Romans 8:1).

In spite of my failure, in spite of the weakness of the flesh and the old nature, in spite of my defeats, *there is no condemnation.* I am still saved. My failures and defeats may bring on the chastening of the Lord, and cause me to "suffer loss" at the Judgment Seat of Christ, but *no condemnation.* Christ has made provision for my security. There is cleansing, deliverance and victory, but no condemnation.

It does not say, "There is no condemnation for the believer *if he keeps the law perfectly.*" Paul had admitted his failure to do that in no uncertain terms in chapter 7. Many would try to read it that way; but it says, "no condemnation to them which are *in Christ Jesus,* who walk not after the flesh, but after the Spirit." There would be absolutely no point in saying there is no condemnation to those who keep the law. That goes without saying, for it is perfectly clear and evident that the law does not condemn those who keep it. The law does not condemn the righteous, but the sinner, and those who break the law.

However, there is no condemnation even for those who *have broken* the law but who are *in Christ Jesus.* Yea, more, there is no condemnation for believers even though they break the law *after* they are saved. Now don't let this startle you. I said that there is no condemnation for those who are *in Christ,* even though they fail to keep the law perfectly. There is chastening, to be sure, if we are disobedient; there is punishment if we stumble and fall; there is a judging of our sin, *but no condem-nation!* If this were not so, then it would mean that each time the believer sins, he would again come under condemnation of the same law and be lost again, and have to be saved all over again. That cannot be. Who is there that can honestly say at the close of day, "This day I have not sinned in either thought, or word, or deed. This day I have kept the whole law of God perfectly, without an evil thought or a hasty word or a selfish act." God has made provision for our sins after we are saved. We have a High Priest interceding, and we can by confession receive cleans-ing. Thank God for this marvelous provision, that

> If we confess our sins, he is faithful and just to forgive us our sins, and to cleanse us from all unrighteousness (I John 1:9).

But No Condemnation!

Before we end this chapter we must point out the reason why there is no condemnation even though we fail as believers. Here it is:

> For the law of the Spirit of life in Christ Jesus hath made me free from the law of sin and death (Romans 8:2).

God sees us *in Christ* as perfect and sinless, and accepts us not on the basis of our own righteousness but the righteousness of Christ. This righteousness the law could not give us. It was way beyond our reach, and our Scripture therefore says:

> For what the law could not do, in that [because] it was weak through the flesh, God sending his own Son in the like-ness of sinful flesh, and for sin, condemned sin in the flesh:
> That the righteousness of the law might be fulfilled *in us*, who walk not after the flesh, but after the Spirit (Romans 8:3, 4).

The fact then that the law cannot save the sinner, nor keep the saint, is not the fault of the law, but of sinful flesh. That which the law could not do, was because of man's sinful nature. And because we could not attain unto righteousness by our own efforts, God sent His Son into the world to satisfy the law for us, by paying its penalty on the cross, and then offering us *His* righteousness, that the righteousness of the law might be fulfilled *in us*. Notice, it does not say that it might be fulfilled *by* us, but *in us.* Have you been trying to make yourself fit for salvation by your own efforts? Have you tried to earn God's favor by doing your best? Oh, friend, your best is not good enough. Why not accept His righteousness, and be able to say:

> I've tried in vain a thousand ways
> My fears to quell, my hopes to raise;
> But what I need, the Bible says,
> Is ever, only Jesus.

Chapter Fifteen

WEAK THROUGH THE FLESH

There are some things the law cannot do. There are sincere but misinformed people who are severely shocked when we make the assertion that the law of God is completely powerless to save a sinner or to keep a saint saved. They remind us that the law of God is perfect and holy and just, to all of which we agree; but while the law is perfect, it cannot produce perfection in imperfect sinners. While the law is holy, it cannot produce holiness in the transgressor. While the law of God is just, it cannot justify injustice and unrighteousness. These things the law cannot do, nor was it ever intended to do. Its ministry is to reveal the perfect righteousness of a holy God; righteousness is the one requirement for salvation, and this the law could not provide. The law may be compared to a yardstick which shows how far short we come of God's perfect standard, but the yardstick cannot correct the deficiency. Paul expresses it perfectly in Romans 8:3, "For what the law could not do. . . ."

To understand what Paul is trying to say we must go back once more to the preceding verses. In chapter 7 of Romans, Paul admits his failure as a believer to keep the law of God perfectly, and ceasing from his own struggle he turns it all over to the Saviour. He cries out:

> O wretched man that I am! who shall deliver me from the body of this death? (Romans 7:24).

And immediately he gives the answer: "I thank God through Jesus Christ our Lord . . ." (Romans 7:25).

What Paul found himself unable to do, he turns over to the One, the only One, who can help him. He candidly admits his failure and adds:

> So then with the mind I myself serve the law of God; but with the flesh the law of sin (Romans 7:25).

With his mind he seeks to keep the law of God. The mind is the "will," and Paul earnestly wants to keep the law perfectly, but finds the flesh, the old nature, opposing him at every turn. He therefore disclaims any perfection of his own, and relies entirely upon the imputed perfection of the Lord Jesus Christ. He rejoices in the fact that even for his failure after he has been saved, the Lord has made provision, and that in spite of his shortcoming,

> There is therefore now no condemnation to them which are in Christ Jesus, who walk not after the flesh, but after the Spirit (Romans 8:1).

No condemnation in Christ! He does not say that this is only for those who keep the law of God perfectly, but rather that there is no condemnation even to those who have broken God's law, and, confessing it, have fled to Christ Jesus for forgiveness. And then Paul says,

> For the law of the Spirit of life in Christ Jesus [grace] hath made me free from the law of sin and death (Romans 8:2).

Paul mentions two laws—the law of sin and death which condemned him, and "the law of the Spirit of life in Christ Jesus" which had removed the condemnation for sin forever. And then comes that remarkable verse:

> For what the law could not do, in that it was weak through the flesh, God sending his own Son in the likeness of sinful flesh, and for sin, condemned sin in the flesh (Romans 8:3).

For what the law could not do! What is Paul referring to? Removal of the curse and condemnation of sin. It was powerless to save the sinner, to justify one single transgressor, or to overlook one single sin. The law says, "the soul that sinneth, it shall die"; "the wages of sin is death"; and he "will by no means clear the guilty." Please notice the language of the law—the wages of sin is death. It does not say "wages of *sins*" but sin—*one single sin* is enough to bring down the curse of the law. It is not the amount of sinning, but the fact of sin which brings damnation. The law demands perfection, and one sin is enough to condemn. James says:

> For whosoever shall keep the whole law, and yet offend
> in one point, he is guilty of all (James 2:10).

Sin is sin. There are no "little sins" and "big sins" in the sight of God. If you think God will overlook a little sin and punish only gross sin, remember Adam and his disobedience in taking what God had forbidden. We would call the act petty larceny, taking a forbidden fruit, but God regarded it as an act of rebellion and His righteousness demanded the maximum penalty of death. For one little(?) sin Moses had to die before he could enter the land of Canaan. The law was given to reveal the real gravity of all sin, and the righteous demands of a holy God and His condemnation of every sin. Now the law could not justify or save these transgressors. This was not the fault of the law, for notice how the verse continues (Romans 8:3),

> For what the law could not do, in that it was *weak*
> through the flesh . . . .

The law was weak *through the flesh*. The law was not weak, but the flesh was weak. I remember many years ago an illustration of this truth, given by that marvelous teacher of grace, Dr. William L. Pettingill. In commenting on this verse, *"weak through the flesh,"* he said something like this: "Try and visualize a woman preparing dinner and placing a roast in the oven to be removed when it was done just right. But just before it was time to turn off the heat, Mrs. I. M. Nosy called on the telephone with a choice bit of juicy news. The cook forgot all about the roast in the oven as the telephone conversation dragged on. Then suddenly she remembered the roast, and quickly hanging up she found the meat completely overcooked and ready to fall apart. She took a fork, plunged it into the roast in an effort to lift it out, but the fork would not hold and slipped out with shreds of meat clinging to it. Again she plunged the fork into the meat, but again, 'whoops,' the fork would not hold." And then Dr. Pettingill said with that characteristic twinkle in his eye, 'You see, the fork was weak through the flesh. The fork was all right. It might have been sterling silver, but it could not rescue the roast, for the flesh was weak.'

"And then the woman had an idea. She laid aside the fork, and instead she took a broad spatula, slipped it under the roast, and lifted it out intact, and in one piece. What the fork could not do in that it was weak through the flesh, the spatula did with ease."

Now that is a rather homely illustration, but if it conveys the meaning of Paul's words, it is worthwhile. The fork may be compared to the law. It is perfect and flawless, but the sinful flesh of man could not be rescued from the flame by its use. The spatula is the grace of God, which did what the law could not do. Now we are ready for the rest of the verse:

> For what the law could not do, in that it was weak through the flesh, *God sending his own son* in the likeness of sinful flesh, and for sin, condemned sin in the flesh (Romans 8:3).

The failure of the law to justify the sinner became the occasion for God stepping in to save the poor, condemned wretch. Notice the wording:

> . . . God sending his own Son in the likeness of sinful flesh [His incarnation], and for sin [His atoning death], condemned sin in the flesh (Romans 8:3).

Notice two things about God's provision for sinners in His Son Jesus Christ. He sent Him in the "likeness of sinful flesh." Christ took on Him our humanity when He was born. Here He took on Himself our human nature, but not our sinful human nature. Paul is careful to say in the "likeness of sinful flesh," and not "in sinful flesh." What an evidence of divine inspiration in guarding the sinlessness of Jesus! He became like unto us in all things (Hebrews 2:17). By His supernatural conception and virgin birth He assumed our human nature, but escaped the guilt of Adam's sin. When the law had failed to justify Adam's race, God sent the Second Man, the last Adam, to redeem poor, lost humanity from the curse of the perfect, holy law of God. But His incarnation, His virgin birth in the "likeness of sinful flesh," was not sufficient to obtain redemption. While He did not share Adam's sin, nevertheless Adam's sin must be taken care of. In order to pay for Adam's sin, every demand of the law must be fully met, for the law will in no wise clear the guilty. Redemption cannot be obtained until the last farthing is paid. The righteous demands of God's holy law must be met, and the penalty borne. This was accomplished when Christ, who was free from Adam's sin, took our sin upon Himself and paid its penalty on Calvary's cross. The prophet Isaiah foresaw this centuries before, and cried:

> All we like sheep have gone astray; we have turned every one to his own way . . . (Isaiah 53:6).

This called for the judgment of God, eternal death and damnation. And then Isaiah continues with,

but

> . . . and [but] the LORD hath laid on him the iniquity of us all (Isaiah 53:6).

The verse begins with the all-inclusive word of condemnation, "*all* have gone astray," and ends with the universal *all* of invitation. Now the statement makes sense, "in the likeness of sinful flesh (the incarnation), and for sin (His death and resurrection)."

This satisfies all the demands of the law. It did not justify or pass over sin, but it "condemned sin in the flesh." The very fact that Jesus had to take upon Him our nature and take our sins to the cross, proves the awfulness of sin, and so Paul says that the "death of Christ" condemned sin in the flesh.

THE RESULT

Now the glorious result in the next verse (Romans 8:4),

> That the righteousness of the law might be fulfilled *in us,* who walk not after the flesh, but after the Spirit (Romans 8:4).

Fulfilled *in* us! It does not say *by* us. Our failure to do this had been proven by God's holy law. This the law was unable to do! Before we were saved we were condemned, having come short of God's righteousness; and He, seeing our lost condition, made a way by which we might be counted righteous in the eyes of the law. This is an imputed righteousness provided by the Lord Jesus Christ. He died to pay the penalty of the law; then He arose to take His own righteousness and clothe the believer with it. The penalty for sin is paid, and now because we are *in Christ,* God looks upon the believer as righteous, complete and perfect. We are justified. He accepts what Christ has done for us, and reckons it to our account, and now as He sees us in Christ, we are,

To the praise of the glory of his grace, wherein he hath made us *accepted in the beloved.*

In whom we have redemption through his blood, the forgiveness of sins, according to the riches of his grace (Ephesians 1:6, 7).

Chapter Sixteen

THE HIGH PRIEST AND THE LAW

For twenty-five hundred years, from Adam to Moses, there was no written law of God. The law written upon tables of stone was given to Moses after the children of Israel had been delivered and redeemed by blood from the bondage of Egypt. For 2500 years man had the light of nature and the light of conscience, but no law to reveal to him the perfect righteousness and holiness of God. Then God gave to Israel through Moses the law. There was a threefold giving of the law. The first time it was orally spoken to Moses on the mount, and communicated by mouth to the children of Israel. Israel accepted that law and promised to keep it perfectly. They answered Moses,

> . . . All that the LORD hath spoken we will do . . .
> (Exodus 19:8).

How little they realized that they were unable to keep God's law perfectly, and that their only hope was to remain under the grace of God which had delivered them from their bondage. Israel in their blindness having proclaimed their ability to keep God's law, the Lord now calls Moses back up the mountain to give him a written copy of that law inscribed upon the tables of stone. This was the second giving of the law.

> And the LORD said unto Moses, Come up to me into the mount, and be there: and I will give thee tables of stone, and a law, and commandments which I have written; that thou mayest teach them.
> And Moses went up into the mount, and a cloud covered the mount.
> . . . and Moses was in the mount forty days and forty nights (Exodus 24:12, 15, 18).
> And he gave unto Moses, when he had made an end of communing with him upon mount Sinai, two tables of testimony, tables of stone, written with the finger of God (Exodus 31:18).

WHY THE FORTY DAYS?

We ask the question, Why did Moses remain in the mountain for forty days? The Lord could have given Moses the two tables of the law immediately and sent him back to deliver them to the children of Israel. We believe there are two reasons for the delay of forty days. These reasons are: (1) to permit Israel to prove that they could *not* keep God's law, even for forty days. They had so arrogantly and confidently boasted, "All that the Lord has commanded, we will do." They must be convinced of their utter sinfulness and inability to please God by their own efforts. See how this is demonstrated by the action of Israel during the absence of Moses for forty days:

> And when the people saw that Moses delayed to come down out of the mount, the people gathered themselves together unto Aaron, and said unto him, Up, make us gods, which shall go before us; for as for this Moses, the man that brought us up out of the land of Egypt, we wot not what is become of him (Exodus 32:1).

The rest of the story of the golden calf is familiar. This people who had heard the word, "Thou shalt have no other gods before me," are now dancing, drinking, carousing, and offering sacrifices to a dead idol. What a demonstration of the wickedness of the human heart! This was the reason Moses was delayed in bringing down the tables of stone. It was to demonstrate that they were unable to serve God perfectly.

There is a second reason for the delay of forty days before Moses returned to the people. It was (2) to make a provision for escaping the judgment of the broken law. According to that law which Moses was to deliver, the immediate death penalty was pronounced. This sin must be atoned for or else the nation must perish. And so at the same time God gave the law which damned, cursed and condemned the transgressor, God also made provision for their redemption from the curse.

THE TABERNACLE

When Moses went up to the mount of Sinai to receive the tables of the law, he received something in addition to the two tables of the decalogue. It was the plan of redemption in the worship of the blood-sprinkled Tabernacle. Observe carefully that between Moses' going up into the mount (Exodus 24:12-18) and his coming down from the mountain (Exodus 32:7), there are *eight chapters* devoted to the pattern of the Tabernacle, God's answer to the broken law. During the forty days Israel was breaking God's law, He was giving Moses His provision for salvation for those who were transgressing those very commandments. Had Moses come down from the mountain with only the tables of the law, it would have been the end of the nation of Israel, but together with the tables of the law came also the message of salvation and redemption by blood. The writer of Hebrews tells us Moses received the pattern of the Tabernacle at the same time he was given the tables of stone. Hebrews tells us:

> . . . Moses was admonished of God when he was about to make the tabernacle: for, See, saith he, that thou make all things according to the pattern shewed to thee in the mount (Hebrews 8:5).

This Tabernacle in the wilderness was a picture, shadow, type and prophecy of the Lord Jesus Christ. This is clear from Hebrews 8:

> Now of the things which we have spoken this is the sum: We have such an high priest, who is set on the right hand of the throne of the Majesty in the heavens;
> A minister of the sanctuary, and of the true tabernacle, which the Lord pitched, and not man (Hebrews 8:1, 2).
> But Christ being come an high priest of good things to come, by a greater and more perfect tabernacle, not made with hands, that is to say, not of this building;
> Neither by the blood of goats and calves, but by his own blood he entered in once into the holy place, having obtained eternal redemption for us (Hebrews 9:11, 12).

The Tabernacle was a type of the Lord Jesus Christ. It was called "the tent of meeting," for here on the basis of the blood, the sinner could come to God. So we repeat, when Moses came down from the mount after forty days, he brought with him two things:

1. The law which condemned the sinners; and
2. The pattern of the Tabernacle pointing to Jesus Christ, the lamb of God which beareth away the sin of the world.

The law condemned the sinner, and Moses in his righteous anger cast the tables of the law upon the rocks, and smashed them in pieces, to dramatize what Israel had already done by their worship of the golden calf. Before Moses could present them with the tables of stone, they had already broken them. But God had anticipated Israel's failure, and so in mercy He provided the Lord Jesus Christ who by His own blood would atone for the broken law, so the transgressors might be spared and not perish.

This provision in the person of the Lord Jesus Christ was symbolized and taught by the pattern and instructions for the Tabernacle which was God's answer to the judgment of the law. Every part of this Tabernacle pointed to God's substitutionary, atoning Lamb, but was climaxed in the Ark of the Covenant in the Holy of Holies.

Third Giving of the Law

Before looking into this ark of the covenant, we must mention the third giving of the law. The tables of stone which God made were broken at the foot of the mount, and the only thing which spared Israel from death was the blueprint of the blood-sprinkled Tabernacle carried by Moses. Now there is to be a third giving of this law:

> And the LORD said unto Moses, Hew thee two tables of stone like unto the first: and I will write upon these tables the words that were in the first tables, which thou brakest.
>
> And be ready in the morning, and come up in the morning unto mount Sinai, . . .
>
> And he [Moses] hewed two tables of stone like unto the first; and Moses rose up early in the morning, and went up unto mount Sinai, as the LORD had commanded him, and took in his hand the two tables of stone (Exodus 34:1, 2, 4).

Now notice what was to be done with this copy of the law. It was to be hidden in the Ark of the Covenant in the Tabernacle. The Ark of the Lord was the central object, the very heart of the Tabernacle teaching. It was a wooden, oblong box, overlaid with gold and covered by a lid of solid gold with two cherubims overshadowing it. In this box or Ark was to be placed these *second* tables of the law—the law which Israel had broken. This law demanded punishment and cried out for justice. And so God placed over this law a lid called the "mercy seat." Within the Ark the law pronounced the sentence of death, but God had provided a covering. The "mercy seat" or cover of the Ark was a picture of the Lord Jesus Christ. He is called our mercy-seat in Romans 3:25. Here we read concerning Christ,

> Whom God hath set forth to be a propitiation through faith in his blood . . . (Romans 3:25).

The word translated "propitiation" is *hilasterion* in the original and means literally "mercy-seat." Upon this mercy-seat covering the broken law which called for the death of the nation, the High Priest, once a year on the day of atonement, took blood from the altar in the Court of the Tabernacle, and sprinkled it upon the mercy-seat over the broken law, and then when God descended in the cloud of shekinah glory into the Holy of Holies, He did not see the broken law, but the blood instead. God Himself had said before,

> . . . when I see the blood, I will pass over you (Exodous 12:13).

All of this was fulfilled by the Lord Jesus Christ. He was here on earth for thirty-three years to prove the same two things Moses proved by his sojourn on the mount for forty days and nights. We said it was to prove two things:
1. The awful sinfulness of the human heart, and the failure of the law to make men better.
2. To demonstrate God's provision of salvation, which the law could not provide.

We remind you again of Paul's statement in Romans 8:3, "For what the law could not do, in that it was weak through the flesh," God did do by sending His Son to deliver us from judgment and death.

The first thing the coming of Christ proved was the exceeding sinfulness of sin. After fifteen hundred years of the thunderings and threatenings of the law, the nation of Israel committed the crime of all time, by condemning to death the only man who had ever kept God's law perfectly, the only One whom the law could not condemn. Now if that were all, God would have been compelled to damn all humanity into Hell forever. But as Moses came from the mount with *two things*, the death-dealing law and the life-giving pattern of the Tabernacle, so Christ's coming also revealed the failure of the law to make men better, but by dying on the cross and shedding His blood He opened a way whereby these same guilty, godless, hopeless, lawless sinners could be declared righteous; for the blood now stands between the believer and God who said,

> . . . When I see the blood, I will pass over you . . . (Exodus 12:13).

We close with the same emphasis with which we began— what the law could not do, Jesus did! By His life and by His death, He condemned sin in the flesh, but at the same time he provided forgiveness for the sinner who will fly to Him in faith.

By the shedding of His blood, by His substitutionary, atoning death and resurrection, the Throne of God which by the law was a throne of judgment and death, became a throne of mercy and life.

What the law could not do, Jesus did!

Chapter Seventeen

THE GOSPEL PREACHED TO ABRAHAM

How were people saved before Jesus died and rose to justify
the believer? How was Adam saved? How was Abraham saved?
Were they saved by the law? This was impossible, for all of
them lived before the giving of the law. Abraham knew absolutely nothing about the Ten Commandments given to Moses
upon Mount Sinai. Clearly the Bible declares that the law was
not given to Israel until four hundred and thirty years after
Abraham was saved (Galatians 3:17). Certainly Abraham was
not saved by keeping the law, nor was he kept saved by it. How
then was Abraham saved? The Bible takes great pain in telling
us. In the first three chapters of Romans Paul had gone to great
lengths to prove that no one ever was saved by works, but by
grace. He comes to the final conclusion in verse 28:

> Therefore we conclude that a man is justified by faith
> without the deeds of the law (Romans 3:28).

This was a difficult truth for his legalistic listeners to accept,
and so Paul refers them to father Abraham, revered and honored
by all. He asks, How was Abraham saved? By the law, or by
grace? Listen to Paul:

> What shall we say then that Abraham our father, as
> pertaining to the flesh, hath found?
> For if Abraham were justified by works, he hath whereof
> to glory; but not before God.
> For what saith the scripture? Abraham believed God, and
> it was counted unto him for righteousness.
> Now to him that worketh is the reward not reckoned of
> grace, but of debt.
> But to him that worketh not, but believeth on him that
> justifieth the ungodly, his faith is counted for righteousness
> (Romans 4:1-5).

118

Abraham was saved by believing, long before the Ten Commandments were written upon tables of stone. How then was he saved? Well, says Paul,

> . . . what saith the scripture? . . . (Romans 4:3).

That is the final word. What does the Scripture say? Was Abraham saved by the law? Listen to the answer:

> . . . Abraham believed God, and it was counted unto him for righteousness (Romans 4:3).

Note carefully, "Abraham believed God." It does not say "Abraham believed *in* God" but he believed God. Now, of course, Abraham believed in God. He could hardly believe God, until he first believed in God.

> . . . he that cometh to God must believe that *he is* [that is fundamental], and that he is a rewarder of them that diligently seek him (Hebrews 11:6).

A person may believe in God and be lost forever, and indeed he will be, if all he does is believe in a God. Only the fool says in his heart, "There is no God." But simply believing in a God, some kind of a God, is not enough. It is well to remember this in these days of much flippant talk about God. Everyone today talks about God, about praying to God, returning to God, putting God back in our nation's life. It is well to remember in all this talk about faith in God, that this is not enough. Abraham *believed God.* He believed what God said, He believed God's Word.

WHAT DID ABRAHAM BELIEVE?

We ask, therefore, What did Abraham believe? He believed not only that God existed, but he believed what God *said.* Abraham believed the *Gospel!* He believed the Gospel, the good news of the virgin birth, the atoning death, and the resurrection of the Lord Jesus Christ. Listen to the inspired words in Galatians 3:

> Even as Abraham believed God [not only *in* God], and it was accounted to him for righteousness.
> Know ye therefore that they which are of faith, the same are the children of Abraham.
> And the scripture, foreseeing that God would justify the

heathen through faith, preached before *the gospel unto Abraham*, saying, In thee shall all nations be blessed.

So then they which be of faith are blessed with faithful Abraham.

For as many as are of the works of the law are under the curse: for it is written, Cursed is every one that continueth not in all things which are written in the book of the law to do them.

But that no man is justified by the law in the sight of God, it is evident: for, The just shall live by faith.

And the law is not of faith: but, The man that doeth them shall live in them (Galatians 3:6-12).

The Gospel

Paul contrasts faith and the law, and proves that Abraham was saved by believing the *Gospel*. To the question, "What did Abraham believe to be justified?" the answer is, "He believed the *Gospel*." To understand what Abraham believed, we must define what we mean by the *Gospel*. The word in the Greek is *evangelium* or "good news." Usually the Gospel is defined as the good news of the death and resurrection based on Paul's words in I Corinthians 15,

. . . that Christ died for our sins according to the scriptures.

And that he was buried, and that he rose again the third day according to the scriptures (I Corinthians 15:3, 4).

This definition is usually accepted for the Gospel, but there is *more* to the *good news* than that. The good news also includes the virgin birth, the incarnation of the Lord Jesus Christ. The birth of Jesus was declared to be the Gospel by the angel on the hills of Judea. The angel announced,

. . . Fear not: for, behold, I bring you good tidings of great joy . . .

For unto you is born this day . . . a Saviour . . . (Luke 2:10, 11).

The word translated "good tidings" is the *Gospel*. It is the same word in the Greek, *evangelium*. Yes, the supernatural birth of Jesus is part of the Gospel.

ABRAHAM AND THE GOSPEL

Now back to Abraham and the Gospel. God revealed to him the message of the Gospel of the miraculous conception and birth, the substitutionary death and the glorious resurrection of the coming Redeemer. Abraham believed in the supernatural conception and miraculous birth of a promised son. God had promised to Abraham a seed, in the birth of a son. God had said, concerning Sarah, Abraham's wife,

> . . . I will bless her, and give thee a son also of her: . . . and she shall be a mother of nations . . . (Genesis 17:16).

But the years dragged on and on and this promise remained unfulfilled until Abraham and Sarah had both long passed the age at which either one, in the natural course of nature, could become parents of a son. Abraham was impotent, and Sarah was sterile. Abraham was 100 years old, and Sarah was 90, when we read:

> Now Abraham and Sarah were old and well stricken in age; and it ceased to be with Sarah after the manner of women (Genesis 18:11).

Sarah had passed the age of childbearing and Abraham was impotent (Romans 4:19; Hebrews 11:11). It was at this time God came and told Abraham that he and Sarah would become parents of the promised son. God said,

> . . . Sarah thy wife shall have a son . . . (Genesis 18:10).

And Abraham believed this word of God, even though it was impossible in the course of nature. It would take a miracle, a supernatural act, to make these two old people parents of a son. Although it was naturally impossible, we read:

> And he [Abraham] believed in the LORD; and he counted it to him for righteousness (Genesis 15:6).

Abraham believed the *Gospel*, the good news of the birth of a promised son by a supernatural birth. The birth of Isaac was as great a supernatural miracle as the virgin birth of Jesus Christ, and Abraham believed it. But there is more to the Gospel than the virgin birth. The next step is the substitutionary death of this promised Son. This part of the Gospel also was preached to Abraham and believed by him. When the miraculously born son, Isaac, had reached maturity (personally, I believe Isaac was thirty-three years old when Abraham was commanded to take him to Mount Moriah and sacrifice him upon the altar). Abraham again believed the Gospel, and in Genesis 22 we have a detailed account of Abraham (type of the Father) taking his son (type of the Lord Jesus Christ) up the mountain, and there potentially and typically offering his son upon the altar. Yes, Abraham believed the Gospel, the good news of the miraculous birth and the substitutionary sacrifice of that same son. For God provided a substitute for Isaac when Abraham took the ram from the bushes and offered him up in the "stead of his son" (Genesis 22:13).

There is, however, another part of the Gospel of good news. It is the resurrection of the miraculously born son, who was sacrificed on the mountain. While Isaac was not literally slain, nevertheless God reckoned it as though it actually occurred. Isaac was only a type of the Lord Jesus, but he himself was in need of a Saviour, and so God provided for him a substitutionary ram to die in his stead. But as far as God was concerned He reckoned it as though Isaac was actually slain. And Abraham also potentially sacrificed his son. To Abraham, Isaac was as good as dead for three whole days, from the time of the command to sacrifice his son until God spared him. And so when God suddenly intervened it was a potential resurrection of the son. Abraham, therefore, believed the Gospel—the miraculous birth, the substitutionary death, and the victorious resurrection after three days. Yes, Abraham believed that while he would have to put his son to death, God would also resurrect him. It had to be that way. How else could God fulfill His promise of the seed? God had promised that in Isaac would his seed be called. But Isaac had no seed; he was not even married when he was to die. If then God is to keep His word, Abraham reasoned, God would have to raise him from the dead after his sacrifice.

THE BIBLE CONFIRMS

This is confirmed by the Word of God. Abraham understood that the death and resurrection of Isaac pointed to the death and resurrection of the Greater Son, the promised seed, of whom

Isaac was only a type. In Genesis 22:13, after he had offered his son and saw him restored, Abraham called the name of that place *Jehovah-Jireh*, the Lord will provide, as it is said unto this day, "In the mount of the LORD it shall be seen" (Genesis 22:14).

Abraham looked ahead and saw in this the *Gospel* of the supernatural birth, the atoning death and the resurrection of the Greater Son of Isaac. If any of you doubt this, then read Hebrews 11:

> By faith Abraham, when he was tried, offered up Isaac: and he that had received the promises offered up his only begotten son.
> Accounting that God was able to raise him up, even from the dead; from whence also he received him in a figure [type] (Hebrews 11:17, 19).

This was the Gospel which Abraham believed and by which he was saved. It had nothing to do with keeping the Ten Commandments, for they were not yet given, and God's plan has never changed. Salvation today is still believing what God says about His only Son, virgin-born, crucified and risen again. Paul says, referring to Abraham's faith,

> Now it was not written for his [Abraham's] sake alone, that it was imputed to him;
> But for us also, to whom it shall be imputed, if we believe on him that raised up Jesus our Lord from the dead;
> Who was delivered for our offences, and was raised again for our justification (Romans 4:23-25).

Salvation is not believing in God, or a God, but believing "the record God gave of His Son" (I John 5:10, 11). Salvation is not by the law or by works of man, but by faith in the virgin-born, crucified, risen Saviour. The law is bad news for the sinner, but the Gospel is the good news of salvation by faith in Jesus Christ.

Chapter Eighteen

GOD'S CONDITION FOR FORGIVENESS

The law is bad news to the sinner. The Gospel is the good news to the believer. The law is God's perfect standard of righteousness, a standard which sinful man cannot attain, for we "are shapen in iniquity and conceived in sin." The law is the declaration of God's justice, while the Gospel is the declaration of God's mercy and grace. Both the law and the Gospel are perfect, but they have entirely different purposes and results, for the law condemns the sinner, while the Gospel justifies, and offers salvation from sin. The law and the Gospel are mutually exclusive. It cannot be partly law and partly grace. There can be no mixing of the two in salvation. Nowhere is it more clearly stated than in Romans 11. Paul had used the history of Israel to illustrate the truth of Grace. He had shown in Romans 9 that God did not choose Israel because of any goodness or merit which He saw in them, but it was by pure grace. Abraham had been chosen in grace; Jacob was chosen in sovereign grace. This was all determined before Jacob was born. God knew beforehand that Jacob was a rascal, and Esau (compared to Jacob) was a gentleman. On the basis of moral behavior Esau far exceeded Jacob in ethical qualities. But to illustrate the grace of God, God chose the worst and the meanest and the unworthiest of the two—Jacob. Listen to the Word:

(For the children being not yet born, neither having done any good or evil, that the purpose of God according to election might stand, not of works, but of him that calleth;)

It was said unto her, The elder [Esau] shall serve the younger [Jacob].

As it is written, Jacob have I loved, but Esau have I hated (Romans 9:11-13).

Does this seem unfair? Paul anticipated this question and says:

124

What shall we say then? Is there unrighteousness with God? God forbid (Romans 9:14).

God is sovereign and no one may say to Him that He is unjust. Daniel expressed it long ago, centuries before Paul wrote, and said:

. . . he [God] doeth according to his will in the army of heaven, and among the inhabitants of the earth: and none can stay his hand, or say unto him, What doest thou? (Daniel 4:35).

Shall puny, sinful man call God's dealings in question? Shall man call God into account for what He does in sovereign grace? Well may we answer this in the words of Paul:

Nay but, O man, who art thou that repliest against God? Shall the thing formed say to him that formed it, Why hast thou made me thus?

Hath not the potter power over the clay, of the same lump to make one vessel unto honour, and another unto dishonour? (Romans 9:20, 21).

ISRAEL CALLED BY GRACE

Israel was chosen by God to be His covenant nation, not on the basis of their superiority or excellence, but by the sovereign grace of God. But there is more. Israel was also *kept* by this same sovereign grace. How miserably the nation failed. Their history is one of rebellion, idolatry and sin, culminating in the rejection of their Messiah at Calvary. Did God cast them away again when they proved themselves unworthy of His grace? If justice had prevailed without mercy, truly this would have been the result, but the same sovereign grace which chose them in the beginning also kept them in spite of their unfaithfulness. Although this chosen nation broke God's law over and over again, God did not cast them off. To be sure, He chastened them, He punished them, He corrected them, He scattered them, but He did not violate His covenant of grace.

HATH GOD CAST AWAY HIS PEOPLE?

Paul asks this question, for it is an important one:

I say then, Hath God cast away his people? God forbid . . .
God hath not cast away his people which he foreknew
(Romans 11:1, 2).

The reason was the unfailing grace of God. If Israel's blessing
as the people of God had depended upon their behavior, all
would have been different, but it was all of grace, and grace
excludes all works. Grace is the undeserved, unmerited favor
to those who are utterly unworthy. If the least bit of works or
human goodness is introduced, it ceases to be the work of God
alone. We repeat, grace and law are mutually exclusive—it is
either all of grace without works, or it is not grace at all. We
recommend for careful, intensive study Paul's statement in Romans 11:6,

And if by grace, then is it no more of works: otherwise
grace is no more grace. But if it be of works, then is it no
more grace: otherwise work is no more work (Romans 11:6).

All of this reference to God's dealing with Israel in grace is
given as an illustration for us that we are not only saved by
grace, but also kept by grace without the works of the law. We
have gone on this excursion into the history of Israel because
there are multitudes of sincere believers who imagine that we are
saved by grace, but then after we are saved we must be kept
saved by our perfect behavior and observing the law of God
without one transgression. But this nullifies the whole blessing of
salvation, for who are they who can say that they continuously
and uninterruptedly live a perfect sinless life in full obedience to
God's law, even after they are saved? Is there a day in your life
when you can say, "This day I have not sinned in thought or
word or deed. I have lived in perfect obedience, doing everything which God has commanded and have not come short of
any of the law's requirements, and perfect demands of holiness"?
Can you say, "This day, every minute of it I have loved the
Lord with all my heart and mind and soul, and my neighbor as
myself. I have not been angry, I have not had any evil thoughts,
I have not coveted or been jealous or been selfish. I have not
injured my neighbor by gossip, or failed to help him in time of
need"? Please step forward if you dare claim this. I candidly
confess that I have never lived a day when in the evening I have
not had to confess, "Oh, Lord, this day I have not been all I

should have been. I have been critical, impatient, and been more concerned with my own comfort than the needs of others. Oh, Lord, I ask forgiveness, I confess my sins and imperfection, and accept thy provision of daily grace and cleansing."

GRACE, NOT LAW

To those who say that our security depends upon our perfect behavior after we are saved, I would ask, Don't you need the grace of God any more? Don't you ever need to confess your failures in your struggle with the old nature—the flesh? Then I fear that you know nothing about either the requirements of God's holy law or the true nature of sin.

It would indeed be a sad situation if every time the Christian failed to measure up to God's perfect commandments, he would be lost again. If the believer is under the law, he would be lost again every time he came short of its perfect demands. Remember, the law condemns sin, and if we are under that law, we would be condemned all over again. But God has also made provision for the believer. Jesus not only delivered us from the curse of the law by dying on the cross, but He keeps us delivered from the condemnation of the law by His presence as our interceding High Priest at the right hand of God. Unfortunately, there are some poor, blind, mistaken people who claim sinless perfection. They tell us the old sinful nature has been eradicated, root and branch, and they never sin any more. To them the Lord Jesus Christ is wasting His time at the right hand of God as our interceding High Priest, for they have nothing to confess, and need no one to intercede for them.

SHALL WE SIN?

This does not mean that we must not strive for holiness. This does not mean that we should not be careful to avoid sin. We *ought not* to sin, but the fact is that as long as we have our sinful nature we *do* sin, and for this God's grace has made provision in the priestly work of our Lord. How clear and unmistakable are the words of the Spirit through John:

> My little children, these things write I unto you, that ye sin not . . . (I John 2:1).

John is writing to believers—born-again children of God. He addresses them as "my little children." To these he writes,

"These things write I unto you, that ye sin not." No Christian has a right to sin; he ought never to sin; but, sad to say, we all too often do. And our Father knew this, too, and so John adds to the warning *not to sin,*

> . . . and [but] if any man sin [still talking to believers], we have an advocate with the Father, Jesus Christ the righteous (I John 2:1).

Thank God for that glorious provision! Without it, it would be of little or no value to be saved in the first place, if provision had not been made to keep us saved to the end. And so we admit our failures, and we grieve over them and long for victory over sin, and yearn for holiness; we do not deny our failure, for we know that in us (that is, in our flesh,) "dwelleth no good thing." The worst thing a believer can do is to close his eyes to the possibility of his sinning, and consequently fail to confess them, and so come under the chastening, scourging hand of our God.

DON'T DENY YOUR SINS

To deny that we have failed is only to deceive ourselves and make God a liar. Listen to what God says:

> If we [believers] say that we have no sin, we deceive ourselves, and the truth is not in us.
> If we [believers] say that we have not sinned, we make him a liar, and his word is not in us (I John 1:8, 10).

What then shall we do? The verse inserted between the two verses (8 and 10) which we have just read, gives the remedy:

> If we confess our sins, he is faithful and just to forgive us our sins, and to cleanse us from all unrighteousness (I John 1:9).

We do not even have to ask Him to forgive our sins, but the only condition is *confession,* and when we confess He forgives. Are we under law? Thank God, no! For then we should come back under condemnation every time we fail, but we are under grace, which makes provision for forgiveness and for cleansing.

Child of God, do you know your own heart in the light of the Word of God? Do you know the true nature of sin? Sin is not only an overt, outward act, but it is primarily an attitude of the heart which fails to put God first in every thought, word and deed. Sin is doing anything independently of God. Do you have a true concept of the holiness of God? To do anything without recognizing God, is sin. In Proverbs 21:4 we read: ". . . the plowing of the wicked, is sin." Failure to recognize God as the giver of the harvest, is sin. In closing, let me give you the confession of one who was one of the most godly, spiritual men in history, and read what he (Job) says:

> If I justify myself, mine own mouth shall condemn me: if I say, I am perfect, it shall also prove me perverse (Job 9:20).

Have you been defeated in your struggle? Have you failed so often, and you are tempted to say, What's the use? Or are you despondent because you think God has cast you off again, and you are no longer saved? Then go to Him, and claim His promise of grace.

> If we confess our sins, he is faithful and just to forgive us our sins, and to cleanse us from *all* unrighteousness (I John 1:9).

Then trust Him, and go on to claim His victory!

Chapter Nineteen

LOVE IS THE ANSWER

What shall we say then? Shall we continue in sin, that grace may abound?

God forbid. How shall we that are dead to sin, live any longer therein? (Romans 6:1, 2).

The Apostle Paul anticipated many questions which would be raised by his teaching of the grace of God and freedom from the law for believers. Paul had taught that the believer in Christ is "delivered" from the law (Romans 7:6); "dead" to the law (Galatians 2:19); and "redeemed" from the curse of the law (Galatians 3:13). He had shown that the sinner cannot be saved by the works of the law, and that the believer cannot be kept by the works of the law. Again and again he repeats, "the believer is not under the law, but under grace" (Romans 6:14, 15).

The legalistic sabbatarians of his day were quick to accuse Paul of preaching a dangerous gospel. They followed him everywhere to undo his preaching of grace. And these attacks have continued to this day against all who teach deliverance from the law by faith. Now we do not teach that the law is not active today in declaring God's righteousness, and in condemning the sinner. But we do teach that those who trust in the finished work of Christ are not only "redeemed from the curse and penalty, but from the law itself." A law without penalties is powerless, and since the penalty of the law was fully borne by Christ the believer is forever delivered from its power. We shall try to answer some of the objections which constantly are raised against this doctrine of "grace to save, and grace to keep."

"It Gives License to Sin"

It is persistently argued by the legalists that the teaching of absolute grace in salvation leads to looseness and carelessness in living. To teach the security of the believer by grace is con-

130

demned by our critics as an encouragement to sin, and even called by some a "damnable" doctrine. When we preach freedom from the law, we are accused of being "lawless," when as a matter of fact we are far more under "law" after we are saved than before, but it is under a different law, a more powerful law, the law of love, instead of the law of commandments. The true believer seeks to keep the law of God, but it is from an entirely different motive. The believer is still obligated to observe God's law, but not as an effort to keep himself saved, or out of fear of punishment.

The believer has a moral obligation to live a holy life, not because the law demands it, but because grace produces it. To say, therefore, that freedom from the law makes one lawless is to show complete ignorance of both the ministry of the law and the power of the grace of God. The only service a believer can render, which is pleasing to God, must be generated by a grateful love for his deliverance. Any service motivated by an effort to escape punishment or fear of losing salvation is wholly rejected by the Lord. The believer must live under the spirit of the law—not by the letter of the law.

The believer is under a new law given to us by the Lord Jesus Himself. It is indeed called the *law of Christ*. It is the law of *love* in contrast to the law of commandments. Paul says in Galatians 2:19, "I am dead to the law, that I might live unto God."

THE LAW OF LOVE

Jesus in speaking to His disciples in John 15, says:

> If ye keep my commandments, ye shall abide in my love; even as I have kept my Father's commandments, and abide in his love (John 15:10).

What commandments is Jesus talking about? Certainly not the Ten Commandments, as so many imagine. He is speaking about a different law of commandments, and explains it in verse 12:

> This is my commandment, That ye love one another, as I have loved you (John 15:12).

This is called by Paul, the law of Christ,

> Bear ye one another's burdens, and so fulfill the *law of*
> *Christ* (Galatians 6:2).

The law of Christ is the law of *love*, the fruit of the new
nature and the Spirit of God. We read again:

> For all the law is fulfilled in one word, even in this; Thou
> shalt *love* thy neighbour as thyself (Galatians 5:14).

The Apostle John says in writing to believers:

> And whatsoever we ask, we receive of him, because we
> keep his commandments, and do those things that are
> pleasing in his sight (I John 3:22).

What commandments is John talking about? Certainly not the
Ten Commandments, for he immediately adds:

> And this is his commandment, That we should believe
> on the name of his Son Jesus Christ, and *love one another*,
> as he gave us commandment (I John 3:23).

We might go on and on to show that while we are delivered
from the law of commandments given by Moses, we are not
left without law; we are not lawless, but are placed under
another higher, more glorious law—the law of love, called also
the "perfect law of liberty" (James 1:25).

LOVE, THE FULFILLING OF LAW

We mention one more Scripture which climaxes it all. Paul
says:

> . . . Love is the fulfilling of the law (Romans 13:10).

Where love is the motive for service, no laws, rules or regulations are ever needed. To use an illustration, imagine a man
employing a servant. To avoid any trouble or misunderstanding,
certain rules and conditions must be agreed upon. The employer
hands to his prospective employee a manual in which the rela-
tionships of employer and servant are set forth. The employer
agrees to pay a certain amount of wages per week, with provision
for sick pay, vacation, coffee breaks, proper working conditions,
and other fringe benefits. The servant or employee agrees to work
forty hours a week, be at work at the appointed time, and
produce a certain amount of work. They sit down at a bargaining
session and an agreement is reached. Failure to abide by the

rules will break the contract, and the employee will either go on strike, or the boss will fire him, as the case may be. The responsibilities of both employer and employee have been spelled out in detail. The servant is under *law*—he received his wages and benefits upon condition of meeting all the responsibilities mentioned and demanded in the contract.

LOVE STEPS IN

Now let us suppose this employee is a young lady, and in the course of events the boss, a bachelor, falls in love with his servant. Finally they decide to marry, and they become husband and wife. She quits her job (not her work) and they move into their new home. The very moment she becomes the wife, she ceases to be a servant. She is no longer under rules, regulations and laws. She is not handed an employee's manual to tell her what is expected of her as a wife. She is in love with her husband, and now she does as much, and even far more, to please her husband as when he was her boss.

She is no longer under law; she does not punch a clock; she has no set of rules to observe; she is free, free to spend all her time pleasing her husband. No demands are made upon her, for she already anticipates all her husband's wishes. She is no more a servant, no more under laws, rules and regulations. But does this make her careless and say, now that I am not any more under law I can do as I please? Ah, no! She is under the law of love.

THE COMMANDMENTS

Love is the fulfilling of the law; where love reigns, no laws are needed. Can you imagine the husband of this erstwhile servant posting a set of Ten Commandments on the wall of the kitchen, to remind his wife constantly of her responsibility to him? Can you imagine this wife faced each morning with this set of laws posted above the kitchen sink? It reads as follows: "Ten Commandments for my wife":

1. Thou shalt entertain no other husbands beside me.
2. Thou shalt not have pictures, photographs, or mementos of other men for thee to worship.
3. Thou shalt not take my name in vain or speak disparagingly about me.
4. Thou shalt not sweep the dirt under the rug.

5. Thou shalt faithfully prepare my meals, see that my laundry is taken care of, etc., etc., etc. All the way down—ten commandments.

Ah, no, a loving wife does not even have to be reminded of these things, for love anticipates all the needs of her lover. She does not have certain working hours, she does not receive wages, although she is on duty twenty-four hours of the day. The husband does not have to say to her, "These are your responsibilities; see that you perform them perfectly; for if you don't, I will punish you or even divorce you." The whole thing is silly. Love makes such a situation unthinkable.

A servant is only expected to do as much as is legally required, only as much as the contract covers; but it is not so with a faithful wife. She goes far beyond what a servant does. So, too, when we are saved by grace and we come under the law of Christ, the law of love, we not only seek to do all that we were required to do under the law of a servant, but go far beyond the demands of the law. The loving wife does not say, "Well, I've done all I am required to do; I've put in my time. Now I am free." Instead, the service of love knows no limits.

Love, then, is the fulfilling of the law; the more love, the less law: and the less love, the more law is needed. All the requirements of the law are met where love rules and controls. Listen to Paul in Romans 13:

> Owe no man any thing, but to love one another: for he that loveth another hath fulfilled the law.
> For this, Thou shalt not commit adultery, Thou shalt not kill, Thou shalt not steal, Thou shalt not bear false witness, Thou shalt not covet; and if there be any other commandment, it is briefly comprehended in this saying, namely, Thou shalt love thy neighbour as thyself.
> Love worketh no ill to his neighbour: therefore love is the fulfilling of the law (Romans 13:8-10).

This same thing was expressed by Jesus in Matthew 19:19 and Mark 12:31, and repeated by Paul in Galatians 5:14,

> For, brethren, ye have been called unto liberty; only use not liberty for an occasion to the flesh, but by love serve one another.
> For all the law is fulfilled in one word, even in this; Thou shalt love thy neighbour as thyself (Galatians 5:13, 14).

Where this rule of love is practiced, there is no more need for any laws. You could discharge every police officer and close every court of law. If you love the Lord God with all your heart and mind and soul, and your neighbor as yourself, the law has no power over you. If you love your neighbor as yourself, you will not commit adultery; if you love your neighbor as yourself you will not kill him; if you love your neighbor as yourself you will not steal from him, you will not bear false witness against him, you will not covet what belongs to him; and, says Paul:

> . . . if there be any other commandment, it is briefly comprehended in this saying, namely, Thou shalt love thy neighbour as thyself (Romans 13:9).

Brother, may I ask you, Are you under the law of commandments or are you motivated by the law of love? But you say, Who is sufficient unto these things? My love is so imperfect, often so cold, and I come so far short. When I fail to be motivated by perfect love, do I then come again under the law of condemnation and the curse? Bless God, no, for He knew our frailty and made provision by His grace for even this, and we repeat once more I John 2:1 and I John 1:8-10,

> My little children, these things write I unto you, that ye sin not. And [but] if any man sin, we have an advocate with the Father, Jesus Christ the righteous (I John 2:1).
> If we say that we [believers] have no sin, we deceive ourselves, and the truth is not in us.
> If we confess our sins, he is faithful and just to forgive us our sins, and to cleanse us from all unrighteousness.
> If we say that we have not sinned, we make him a liar, and his word is not in us (I John 1:8-10).

Chapter Twenty

THE DIVINE TEACHER

O foolish Galatians, who hath bewitched you, that ye should not obey the truth, before whose eyes Jesus Christ hath been evidently set forth, crucified among you?

This only would I learn of you, Received ye the Spirit by the works of the law, or by the hearing of faith?

Are ye so foolish? having begun in the Spirit, are ye now made perfect by the flesh? (Galatians 3:1-3).

The Apostle Paul had preached salvation through faith by the grace of God without the works of the law. Many in the region of Galatia were happy in their new-found redemption and their complete freedom from the curse of the law. But then certain legalistic Judaistic sabbatarians, who made a practice of following Paul everywhere he went, also came to Galatia and began to teach these happy new converts that Paul was all wrong in preaching salvation by grace alone. They agreed with Paul that one is saved by grace without the works of the law, but then after that he must be kept saved by his works and his perfect obedience to the commandments of God. This greatly disturbed the Galatian Christians who evidently knew that they needed God's grace to keep them, as well as to save them. But these legalists kept hammering away until the churches of Galatia were all confused.

PAUL TO THE RESCUE

The reports of this confusion reached the ears of Paul while he was preaching in the city of Corinth, and he immediately wrote this epistle under inspiration and dispatched it to the churches of Galatia to correct the error. The error was the teaching that we are saved by grace, and then we are kept saved by our behavior and keeping of the law. Paul's answer is that salvation is all of grace: saved by grace, kept by grace. In our Scripture in Galatians 3, Paul expresses both surprise and indignation at the fickleness of these converts and says:

136

O foolish Galatians, who hath bewitched you . . . (Galatians 3:1).

Then he asks two questions. First, how were you saved? This is in verse 2:

This only would I learn of you, Received ye the Spirit by the works of the law, or by the hearing of faith? (Galatians 3:2).

The answer, of course, was *by faith*, and not by the works of the law. Then follows the second question:

Are ye so foolish? having begun in the Spirit, are ye now made perfect by the flesh? (Galatians 3:3).

How foolish can you be? If our God of grace by His mercy and love was willing to save us when we were ungodly sinners, will He not continue to love us enough after we are His children, to keep us unto the end? It is utterly unthinkable that God would sacrifice His Son for sinners and then cast off His children. Let us ask Paul what he thinks about this. He has already clearly expressed himself in Galatians 3:1-3, but listen to him now as he writes to the Philippians:

Being confident of this very thing, that he which hath begun a good work in you will perform it until the day of Jesus Christ (Philippians 1:6).

This was the confidence Paul had for the Philippian Christians, and this same confidence he also had for himself. Listen to his testimony to Timothy:

. . . for I know whom I have believed, and am persuaded that he is able to keep that which I have committed unto him against that day (II Timothy 1:12).

Paul had no fear of losing his salvation. However, he did fear, greatly fear, that he might fail the Lord and be chastened and lose his reward and become a castaway (disapproved for the desired crown), but he did not fear that the Lord would be unfaithful. We repeat, Paul never doubted the faithfulness of God, but he was disturbed by the possibility of *his* failing the Lord. (Read carefully I Corinthians 9:24-27.)

In Romans 8:33 Paul asks one of his striking questions so characteristic of him. It is a challenge:

> Who shall lay anything to the charge of God's elect? It is God that justifieth.
>
> Who is he that condemneth? It is Christ that died, yea rather, that is risen again, who is even at the right hand of God, who also maketh intercession for us (Romans 8:33, 34).

If you will look at these verses carefully in your Bible, you will notice that there are two little words in verse 33, and the same two little words in verse 34, which are written in italics. The italicized words were added by the translators, but are not found in the original. Such words were supplied to make sense, but in some cases they obscure the sense instead. Read Romans 8:33, 34, and omit the two words, "It is," and you will get the real force of the passage:

> Who shall lay anything to the charge of God's elect? (Romans 8:33).

Now omit the words "It is," and we read this: *God that justifieth?* Preposterous! Will God who justified us now afterwards charge us again? Now in verse 34, omit again the two words, "It is," and we read it thus:

> Who is he that condemneth? *Christ that died?*

Will He now condemn us? He who died for us to save us, will He now again condemn us? Christ who is risen from the grave and ascended into Heaven, will He condemn us now? He who sits at God's hand to make intercession for us, will He condemn us? Is He sitting at God's right hand placing His children under the condemnation of the law every time they stumble and fall? Of course not! He is there to make intercession for us. And so we ask again, "Who is he that condemneth?" Christ who died and rose and intercedes? Will He condemn us? Perish the thought! How hopeless would be our estate if this were so.

The Conclusion

No wonder Paul breaks out in a paean of victory and a burst of praise and cries out:

> Who shall separate us from the love of Christ? shall tribulation, or distress, or persecution, or famine, or nakedness, or peril, or sword?
>
> Nay, in all these things we are more than conquerors through him that loved us.

For I am persuaded, that neither death, nor life, nor angels, nor principalities, nor powers, nor things persent, nor things to come,

Nor height, nor depth, nor any other creature, shall be able to separate us from the love of God which is in Christ Jesus our Lord (Romans 8:35, 37-39).

No, says Paul, we cannot be separated by death, life, angels, height or depth. But says one of our dear brethren who seem to be afraid of such security, "These things may not be able to separate us, but we ourselves, we can separate *ourselves* and lose our salvation." Well, Paul evidently anticipated that objection, and so, enumerating all the things which cannot separate us, he then adds, *nor any other creature*, and that included us, *you* and *me*.

YOUR OBJECTION, PLEASE?

The believer then is free and delivered forever from the curse and condemnation of the law. One of the most frequent objections raised to this teaching is a passage in Matthew 5. It is constantly used to prove we are still under the law.

Think not that I am come to destroy the law, or the prophets: I am not come to destroy, but to fulfil.

For verily I say unto you, Till heaven and earth pass, one jot or one tittle shall in no wise pass from the law, till all be fulfilled (Matthew 5:17, 18).

Of course, Jesus did not destroy the law, nor do we. Instead we preach that Christ *fulfilled* the law by meeting its demands and paying its penalty for the believer and now that believer is,

. . . delivered from the law, that being dead wherein we were held; that we should serve in newness of spirit [the new law of Christ], and not in the oldness of the letter [the law of commandments] (Romans 7:6).

But, says another, the Bible says that no part of the law shall fail while heaven and earth remain. They quote Luke 16:17,

And it is easier for heaven and earth to pass, than one tittle of the law to fail (Luke 16:17).

But the law has not failed. It succeeded in doing what it was intended to do—reveal sin as a transgression and condemn the sinner. It did its perfect work, and having done its perfect work, left all men under condemnation; but Jesus Christ came to do what the law could not do.

> But when the fulness of the time was come, God sent forth his Son, made of a woman, made under the law,
> To redeem them that were under the law, that we might receive the adoption of sons (Galatians 4:4, 5).

But now someone comes and says, why did you stop at verse 18 of Matthew 5, and not read the rest?

> Whosoever therefore shall break one of these least commandments, and shall teach men so, he shall be called the least in the kingdom of heaven: but whosoever shall do and teach them, the same shall be called great in the kingdom of heaven (Matthew 5:19).

No one in his right mind teaches men to break God's laws. The law still condemns the sinner and exacts its penalty, but for the believer Christ has born the curse of the law, and now the grace of God teaches us holiness, obedience and godliness. The believer desires to keep God's will perfectly, even though he too often is overcome.

THE LAW OUR GUIDE

But here is another objection. "Yes," says one, "I agree that we are justified by faith through grace and not of works; but while we are not under law for salvation, do we not need the law to show us how to live and teach what is right and wrong for us as believers?" Now, that is a legitimate question, but the answer is clear from the Scripture. The believer has within him another guide, a new teacher. When the sinner receives Jesus Christ as Saviour, he is born *from above*, born of the Spirit. The Holy Spirit moves in and takes up His abode within this believer. We become temples of the Holy Spirit, and He is there to guide us into all truth. Jesus said:

> Howbeit when he, the Spirit of truth, is come, he will guide you into all truth . . . (John 16:13).

Nowhere in the New Testament is the law said to be the guide for the believer. He has a better guide, even the *grace of God*. When a question of right or wrong comes up, the believer does not have to run to Exodus 20 to see what the Ten Commandments say about it. Listen to the words of Paul in Titus:

> For the grace of God that bringeth salvation hath appeared to all men,
> Teaching us that, denying ungodliness and worldly lusts, we should live soberly, righteously, and godly, in this present world (Titus 2:11, 12).

It is the grace of God which teaches us how to walk pleasing to Him. How would it sound if we read the verse this way: "For the law of Moses that condemneth the transgressor hath appeared, teaching us that, denying ungodliness . . ."? No, No! It is not the law which is said to teach us, but the *grace of God* is our teacher.

Our guide is not only a set of commandments, but a Person who creates in us a desire to serve the Lord by asking the one question, "Can I do this to the glory of God?" If the answer is no, it is wrong. Everything must be weighed in the balance of God's will.

> Whether therefore ye eat, or drink, or whatsoever ye do, do all to the glory of God (I Corinthians 10:31).

To the Colossians Paul laid down the rule which cannot possibly be misinterpreted or misunderstood:

> And whatsoever ye do in word or deed, do all in the name of the Lord Jesus, giving thanks to God and the Father by him.
> And whatsoever ye do, do it heartily, as to the Lord, and not unto men (Colossians 3:17, 23).

When faced with the problem of whether to do, or not to do a thing, ask yourself the question, "Can I do this to the glory of God? Will it meet with His approval? Would I want to be doing this if Jesus should come?" Oh, beloved, we should have no trouble knowing God's will, if we really are in earnest to please Him because of our perfect redemption through the work of the Lord Jesus. Whatsoever is not of faith is sin.

Chapter Twenty-One

A LIVING SACRIFICE

> Wherefore, my beloved, as ye have always obeyed, not as in my presence only, but now much more in my absence, work out your own salvation with fear and trembling.
>
> For it is God which worketh in you both to will and to do of his good pleasure (Philippians 2:12, 13).

The greatest deception which Satan, the enemy of our souls, has ever foisted upon humanity is the false but appealing doctrine that man can do something to earn his own salvation, by keeping the law of God. The second greatest error is the teaching that we don't have to do anything *after* we are saved. The first error says it makes no difference what you believe, just so you live right, and the second error teaches that it makes no difference how you live, just so you believe right. Both are a delusion and a snare of the enemy.

It is ever faith, followed by works. Faith is the *root* of salvation, but works are the *fruit* of our salvation. God sees our faith, without works, and justifies us on the basis of our faith in His promise. Men, however, will never recognize our faith until they can see it evidenced in our works. God looks at our faith. People can only see our works. Justification is the work of God; our works are the proof to our fellow men of God's work in us. Therefore Paul says,

Work *out* your own salvation.

He does not say work *for* your salvation, but we are to work *out* what God has already worked in. But while believers are not saved or kept by works, God does expect and claim our complete devotion. Paul makes an impassioned plea to the Christians in Rome that they make a full surrender of their lives on the basis of their great salvation.

> I beseech you therefore, brethren, by the mercies of God, that ye present your bodies a living sacrifice, holy,

acceptable unto God, which is your reasonable service (Romans 12:1).

Please note the form of the appeal. It is the language of the grace of God. He says, I *beseech* you. It is not, I command you. This is not on legal ground, but in the realm of grace. It must be a voluntary service, motivated by gratitude and not by constraint or fear of punishment. This is implied by the word, *therefore*. He says, "I beseech you *therefore*." Whenever you come across the word, *therefore*, in the Bible, you should stop and ask, "What is it there for?" It always refers us back to a "wherefore." It points us back to the reason for the plea, "I beseech you therefore." This verse in Romans 12:1 should logically follow Romans 8:35-39.

THE PARENTHESIS

The 9th, 10th and 11th chapters of Romans are a parenthesis between chapters 8 and 12. They are inserted between the closing verse of chapter 8 and the opening verse of chapter 12, as an illustration of the free grace of God. After Paul had shown that we are not only saved by grace, but kept by grace, he stops to call attention to the history of the nation of Israel as an illustration of this truth. The nation had been chosen of God by grace in the covenant which God made with Abraham, Isaac, and Jacob. Then they were placed under the law with its condemnation; but they failed to keep this law and fell into idolatry, bringing upon themselves the chastening of the Lord, and were scattered over the face of the whole earth. They have been there for 2500 years. However, God has not cast them away, or permanently forsaken them, but remembers His covenant and will restore them again and fulfill every covenant promise made to them. The three chapters (Romans 9, 10, and 11) are inserted to illustrate that even when God's people forsake Him, He does not cast them off, but keeps His covenant promise of grace. This is the teaching of the parenthesis (Romans 9-11) between chapters 8 and 12.

In Romans 9 we have Israel's past: her beginning, and her calling in sovereign grace. It is all gathered up in that verse of sovereign choice:

As it is written, Jacob have I loved, but Esau have I hated (Romans 9:13).

It was grace and grace alone. But Israel failed and so God comes to chasten them. Romans 10 is the picture of Israel during this dispensation of their dispersion. It does indeed seem as if God has forsaken them. Today God is not dealing with Israel as a nation. They are set aside. Today the individual Jew can be saved just like the Gentile and by it become a member of the Body of Christ, but the nation is rejected and set aside. This brings us to Romans 11. Is this setting aside of Israel permanent? Has God, who chose the nation in grace, now disowned them and cast them away because they failed? This Paul answers in unmistakable words:

> I say then, Hath God cast away his people? God forbid. For I also am an Israelite, of the seed of Abraham. . . .
> God hath not cast away his people which he foreknew (Romans 11:1, 2).

Just because Israel failed completely to keep God's law, and ended up by the rejection of the Messiah, this did not affect *God's faithfulness*. To be sure, they suffered indescribably for their sin, but God did not disown them or repudiate His covenant of grace. And so after asking, "Hath God cast away his people (Israel)?" he clinches the answer in Romans 11:25,

> For I would not, brethren, that ye should be ignorant of this mystery, lest ye should be wise in your own conceits; that blindness in part is happened to Israel, *until* the fulness of the Gentiles be come in.
> And so all Israel shall be saved: as it is written, There shall come out of Sion the Deliverer, and shall turn away ungodliness from Jacob:
> For this is my covenant unto them, when I shall take away their sins (Romans 11:25-27).

This is the message of Romans 9, 10, and 11. God's people, called in grace, proved themselves unworthy, were chastened of the Lord, but it did not affect their covenant relationship with God, for He is faithful to His word, and will never cast them off, because He is a God of grace. Now remember this section (Romans 9, 10, and 11) is a parenthesis. God's dealing with Israel is an illustration of God's dealing with us in grace. We were saved by grace apart from the works of the law. But what if we fail after we are saved, and fall into sin and disobedience? Does God then cast us off again? Paul had answered this in Romans 8 when he says,

> For I am persuaded, that neither death, nor life, nor angels, nor principalities, nor powers, nor things present, nor things to come,
> Nor height, nor depth, nor any other creature, shall be able to separate us from the love of God which is in Christ Jesus our Lord (Romans 8:38, 39).

It is because of this *security*, this faithfulness of God, that Paul opens Romans 12 with the impassioned plea,

> I beseech you therefore, brethren, by the mercies of God . . . (Romans 12:1).

God's faithfulness becomes the incentive and motive of our surrender to Him, and this faithfulness is illustrated for us in His dealing with the nation of Israel; hence the parenthesis between chapters 8 and 12.

BY THE MERCIES OF GOD

So we go back to Romans 12:1. Paul pleads on the basis of the faithfulness of God, that we yield ourselves to Him. We have already pointed out that it is a plea, not a command. He says, "I beseech you." It is the language of *grace*, and not *law*. Notice next, he is speaking to *believers*. He says "brethren." They were born-again believers but living selfish lives. They were not fully yielded to Him. He is not talking to people who had attained sinless perfection. Now notice what Paul asks these believers to do, not by threat, but by the *mercies of God*:

> . . . that ye present your bodies a living sacrifice, holy, acceptable unto God, which is your reasonable service (Romans 12:1).

This might be paraphrased, "Make me a present of your body, to be used by me as an expression of your gratitude for the mercies I have shown you." God wants us to yield our bodies to Him. So many of us have presented our souls in service to Him, and have been faithful in worship and devotion and prayer, but have withheld our bodies. And notice, He asks us to "present these bodies a *living* sacrifice," or "a sacrifice while we are still alive." I imagine Paul means, while your body is full of life, not only after it is worn out and broken. There are thousands of believers who, I am sure, would die for Christ rather than renounce their faith, but these same Christians are *not* living for Him. God is not asking us to *die* for Him, as others have, but He asks us to *live* for Him. He died for us, and because He died for us, we live for Him. What could be more reasonable than that we should dedicate these lives fully to His service.

The Body Has Members

So many of God's dear people, who do not yet realize the power of complete yielding of their members to Christ, are still seeking for victory in the strength of the flesh, under the fear of the law. Stop your vain struggling and confess that you do fail and then turn to the only One who alone can give victory. Here is the answer to your defeat:

> I beseech you therefore [because of His mercy to you], that ye present your bodies [wholly to him].

Have you ever said to your Lord since you were saved, "Here is my body, dear Lord; from now on it shall be wholly thine"? And remember that body is made of members. Will you say, Lord, here are my eyes, which have been so enamored by the scenes of this world; take them and open them to the need of seeking out the lost, in reading and studying thy word, instead of looking at the silly trash of this age.

Lord, take my ears, that have been so given to listening to the jargon and clamor of a sinful world, so eager to listen to gossip and slander—take these ears and open them to the cry of lost humanity, to listen only for Thy voice, and close them to the things which defile and pollute my mind and my soul.

Take these lips of mine, and this tongue which has so often been used to cut and wound and hurt, and which has been spent in idle gossip and foolish jesting, and cleanse it by my confession, that henceforth this tongue shall speak and repeat only the things which are pure and holy, instead of inflicting injury. Take these hands which have been so grasping for filthy lucre. Take my feet which have so often walked in self-chosen ways and lead them to some soul for Thee. Take my heart, my mind, my will, yea, my every thought and imagination, and make it subject to Thy will. Take my stubborn will, my unwillingness to forgive, and teach me true humility. What is it, my friend, that you have held back from Him who gave His all for you?

REASONABLE SERVICE

Paul calls it your "reasonable service." Notice the words: "present your bodies, holy, acceptable to God, which is your reasonable service." Is it unreasonable of the Lord to ask you for your body to live for Him, when He gave His body on the cross for you? The Lord asks each one, "In the light of what I have done for you, in saving you from Hell, delivering you from the curse and condemnation of the law, and setting you free in the liberty of grace, is it an unreasonable request to ask you to live for Me?"

In closing, we must again remind you, this service is not on the basis of law, but grace. We are not to serve the Lord in order to keep saved, or to escape chastening and punishment, but instead we are to serve Him because we *are* saved, and kept and secure. I want to say it graciously, but I must say it. I often pity those poor professing Christians who behave themselves because of the fear of God's judgment and chastening. Paul could say, "the love of Christ constraineth me," not the law of God threatens me.

I truly pity those sincere souls who live a life of bondage, abstaining from this thing and that thing, and observing this commandment and that commandment, keeping this day holy rather than another, because they fear they will be lost again if they don't live a perfect life. Let me repeat this truth. My heart goes out to those poor souls who must hold themselves in bondage and restraint because they fear losing their salvation if they should fail. That is a low, mean, unworthy motive for serving the Lord. He wants us to serve Him through love, not fear; from a heart of gratitude which rejoices in doing the things that please Him, who pleased not Himself but gave His all to redeem us.

I don't want my children to obey and respect me because they fear a thrashing if they don't; but instead, I want their love and gratitude for that which I have tried to do for them. How much more we should seek those things which are pleasing to Him, and bring forth,

. . . the fruit of the Spirit . . . love, joy, peace, longsuffering, gentleness, goodness, faith,

Meekness, temperance: *against such there is no law*
(Galatians 5:22, 23).

Chapter Twenty-Two

STUMBLING BLOCK OR STEPPING STONE

Stand fast therefore in the liberty wherewith Christ hath made us free, and be not entangled again with the yoke of bondage.

Christ is become of no effect unto you, whosoever of you are justified by the law; ye are fallen from grace (Galatians 5:1, 4).

If there was anything which Paul was dead set against, and would not tolerate for one single moment, it was being placed back under the law from which he had been delivered by the grace of God. He insisted that he was leading the life of victory in Christ. His life was no more governed by the demands of the law, but the constraining power of the love of Christ. He says in I Corinthians:

All things are lawful for me, but all things are not expedient: all things are lawful for me, but all things edify not (I Corinthians 10:23).

"I am not under the law," says Paul. "All things are lawful for me." Four times in this one epistle he makes that statement—"All things are lawful to me." Paul says, "As far as the law is concerned, I am free." Now don't misunderstand this statement. Paul was not free to do as he pleased, but he was free to please God. The law of love has no limitations. It does more than the law of commandments ever required.

What Is This Liberty

This liberty has its definite responsibilities. We cannot exercise our liberty without considering others besides ourselves. There may be things in our lives which are entirely innocent, which we feel at liberty to enjoy, and against which there is no prohibition in the Word of God. Yet this liberty of ours may become a sin, if we fail to seriously consider its effect upon others. As an example, we take Paul who said, "All things are

149

Law or Grace

lawful unto me, but all things are not expedient." The particular question Paul refers to, involved the eating of certain foods. Some of the believers had no guilty conscience about buying and eating legally unclean foods, foods offered to idols, or dining in a pagan temple. But some did not agree with Paul, and thought it was wrong to eat foods prohibited by the law of Moses, and to patronize a heathen temple.

Probably the fact that the church at Corinth consisted of both Jews and Gentiles accentuated this disagreement. The distinction between clean and unclean meats had for centuries been an effective barrier to fellowship between Jews and Gentiles. That wall of partition was done away in Christ, but all the Christians were not fully aware of this liberty. The Gentile Christians in Corinth would see no harm in eating legally unclean foods, but for the Christian Jews it was not so easy, after living for centuries under the law. The difference became a real source of controversy. Who was right? Was it right or wrong to eat legally unclean meats or even clean meats previously offered to idols, and to sit among pagans in an idol's temple to eat?

Paul's Answer

Paul's answer is one which must still be learned by many Christians. He says that as far as he is concerned, he can see no harm in purchasing and buying this meat in an idol's temple. We are not under law, but grace. This meat was probably of far superior quality because only the best was accepted for sacrifice to idols. After the pagan priest had accepted this sacrificial meat, it was then put on sale or served at meals in the temple restaurant. It could probably be bought very reasonably because it had cost the priests nothing. It was given as an offering. Why not take advantage of this saving? However, if you feel it is wrong, don't eat it, says Paul. It really makes no difference. Listen to Paul's words:

> But meat commendeth us not to God: for neither, if we eat [that is, these meats offered to idols], are we the better; neither, if we eat not, are we the worse (I Corinthians 8:8).

Let every man be persuaded in his own mind. But as for me, says Paul,

All things are lawful for me, . . .

Whatsoever is sold in the shambles [the butcher shop], that eat, asking no question for conscience sake:

If any of them that believe not [an unbeliever] bid you to a feast, and ye be disposed to go; whatsoever is set before you, eat, asking no question for conscience sake (I Corinthians 10:23, 25, 27).

Here then is the answer. We are not under legal restraint— we have perfect liberty. Paul says in Romans 14:14,

I know, and am persuaded by the Lord Jesus that there is nothing unclean of itself (Romans 14:14).

But! But! But!

But this is only half the story. If this liberty of ours becomes a stumblingblock to other sensitive, critical believers who think it is wrong, then our insistence upon our liberty becomes a sin. The natural tendency is to defend our liberty, and we are tempted to say, "It's none of your business what I do! My conscience does not forbid me to do this. I am not under law, but live in the liberty of grace and you have no right to sit in judgment upon me." This, says Paul, is making your liberty under grace a sin against your brother. For while we are not under the law of commandments, we are under the law of love and consideration toward others. Listen to Paul. He says, You may have a perfectly clear conscience in regard to this matter of meats offered to idols, *but,*

. . . there is not in every man that knowledge: for some with conscience of the idol unto this hour eat it as a thing offered unto an idol; and their conscience being weak is defiled (I Corinthians 8:7).

There were those, who because of early training or national background, were much opposed to these unclean meats and were terribly offended by those who, like Paul, saw no harm in it. For the sake of these weak brethren who are offended by our liberty, we should be willing to forgo and give up our liberty, lest we cause them to be offended, or encourage them to take the same liberty *against their own conscience.* In other words, "if you see no harm in it, go ahead and eat it, but if you think it is wrong, don't do it," for

> . . . meat commendeth us not to God: for neither, if we
> eat, are we the better; neither, if we eat not, are we the
> worse (I Corinthians 8:8).

Well, you say, that should settle it. It's very simple; let each one do as he pleases, for we are not under law but under grace. But it isn't that simple, for another law should govern our conduct—the law of love. And this law should work both ways. It is a two-way street. First, those who feel that what they are doing is not displeasing to God, have the liberty to do so. But if it offends a weaker brother, the law of love should make us willing to sacrifice our liberty, and refrain from anything that would cause another to stumble.

Second, those who do not agree with the liberties which some Christians enjoy should not sit in judgment or condemn them just because they do not see eye to eye. I am bold to assert that if the teaching of the Word in this matter were practiced, 95 per cent of church troubles could be solved without serious disagreement. There are two prongs to this weapon. They are both clearly stated in Romans 14:13—

> Let us not therefore judge one another any more: but
> judge this rather, that no man put a stumblingblock or an
> occasion to fall in his brother's way.

How wonderful if these instructions could be followed by all of us! First let us refrain from sitting in judgment upon a brother's liberty in Christ. If you feel that your brother is doing things which you think are wrong, then don't do them, but don't condemn your brother. This, of course, never applies to those things which are strictly forbidden in the Bible, but I am referring to matters whereon the Bible is silent and each one must decide for himself. So, let us determine by God's Grace, "I will not sit in judgment upon my brother's honest convictions of conduct." And now comes the other side of the story. Neither are we who feel at liberty in things which we allow, to insist upon continuing them if we know it offends a disagreeing brother. To say, "I see no wrong in this," and disregard what it does to another's conscience is to make your liberty a sin and a stumblingblock.

> But when ye sin so against the brethren, and wound their
> weak conscience, ye sin against Christ.
> Wherefore, if meat make my brother to offend, I will eat

no flesh while the world standeth, lest I make my brother
to offend (I Corinthians 8:12, 13).

What an example! Personally Paul saw no harm in eating in a
worldly pagan temple, and partaking of the food offered to
idols. All things were lawful to him, but if his doing so became an
offense to another or injured his testimony, he would gladly
surrender his right for the sake of his testimony for Christ. Let
us like Paul refrain from every appearance of evil, even though
it means personal sacrifice, and then on the other hand, let us
refrain from judging others who may themselves not practice
this grace.

> But take heed lest by any means this liberty of yours
> become a stumblingblock to them that are weak (I Corin-
> thians 8:9).

How Far Should We Go?

Now I anticipate a question which must be answered. It is
well and good to surrender our personal liberties for the sake of
our testimony but how far must we carry this thing in order not
to be an offense? To what extent must we sacrifice our liberty
to please our neighbor and not injure their weak conscience?
Some people object to the wearing of jewelry, gold rings and
ornaments. Others object to innocent amusements and play in
which we personally see no wrong. There are those who object
to a Christian with a pale complexion using a bit of rouge or
powder; some object to articles of dress with which to adorn the
temple of the Holy Spirit. Some are offended by our supporting
certain projects, others object to the friends we keep, the places
where we eat or seek relaxation and entertainment. There are
those who are offended by the use of coffee, tea and what not.
How far must we go in our efforts not to offend? That will
depend on the amount of grace you have in your heart. The
more grace, the less you will insist on your own liberty, and the
more you will be willing to say with Paul,

> Wherefore, if meat make my brother to offend, I will eat
> no flesh [meat] while the world standeth, lest I make my
> brother to offend (I Corinthians 8:13).

On the other hand, it is equally wrong to sit in judgment
upon these things in other people's lives with which we do not

agree. We may judge sin—sins which are strictly forbidden or implied in the Bible, but on these other questionable matters, mere differences of opinion, we should be gracious: (1) not to judge one another; and (2) not to indulge in practices which will injure another's conscience. Yes, you say, but how far must we carry this matter of yielding to some of these critical fault-finding saints? That, my brother, is a matter for you to decide—just how far to carry this. A safe rule is given in Romans 15,

> We then that are strong ought to bear the infirmities of the weak, and not to please ourselves.
> Let every one of us please his neighbour for his good to edification.
> For even Christ pleased not himself; but, as it is written, The reproaches of them that reproached thee fell on me (Romans 15:1-3).

Having said this, we must admit even this has its limitations. There are some of God's touchy saints who in their legal attitude are so unreasonable in their condemnation of everything we do, that they will find fault no matter what we do. There are some people whom no one can please. It is impossible to get along with them, try as we will. For these cases I thank God every day of my life for one verse in the Bible, the words of Paul in Romans 12:18,

> If it be possible, as much as lieth in you, live peaceably with all men (Romans 12:18).

How I do thank God for those words! Some folks are just impossible, and so we thank God for this word, "If it be possible, as much as lieth in you."

As we conclude this series on *Law or Grace*, I would ask each one, "Are you under law or under grace? Is your conduct one which insists on your legal rights, or is it motivated by the law of love?" All we need ask in any case of doubt concerning the right or wrong of a thing is, "Does it please God, does it help or hinder my testimony, is it what Jesus would do?" To honestly make this the test of conduct will meet the demands of the law, for "love is the fulfilling of the law" (Romans 13:10).

> Hast thou faith? have it to thyself before God. Happy is he that condemneth not himself in that thing which he alloweth (Romans 14:22).

Chapter Twenty-Three

PAYDAY IS COMING

What shall we say then? Shall we continue in sin, that grace may abound? (Romans 6:1).

This was the anticipated question prompted by the closing verses of Romans 5. In the fifth chapter of Romans Paul had reiterated his unalterable conviction that salvation is by grace, plus nothing, minus nothing. He had stated it in Romans 3:28,

Therefore we conclude that a man is justified by faith without the deeds of the law.

This he repeats over and over again and we read in Romans 5:1,

Therefore being justified by faith, we have peace with God through our Lord Jesus Christ.

Paul does not stop here, but he goes on to show that we are not only justified for the present, by faith in Jesus Christ, but it is forever and forever. We are justified once for all, never to come under condemnation again. This is the message of the Gospel, of the death and the resurrection of the Lord Jesus Christ. By His death the Lord Jesus paid the penalty for our sins, by bearing the curse of the law for us on the cross. By His resurrection He proved that the penalty of death had been paid. Had one single sin remained unatoned for, Jesus would still be in the grave in Palestine, for "the wages of sin (one sin, one single sin) is death." The resurrection, therefore, was the proof and the evidence that all sin, every sin, had been paid for, and atoned for. It is well to contemplate this simple and yet important fact. The resurrection, we repeat, is the proof that all our sins were paid by Him. One sin would have kept Christ in the tomb forever.

Because of this, He has provided for us a perfect righteousness, in which we are now clothed, and we stand before God justified, "just as if we had never sinned." And this is the reason that we are eternally secure. If you still have trouble believing this, then let me ask you, "How long ago did Jesus die for your sins?" It was long before you were even born. It was long before you had ever committed a single sin. How many of these sins did He die for nineteen hundred years ago? For only part of them, or for all of them? It is a question to ponder. Did Jesus die only for those sins which He knew we would commit before we were saved, or also for the sins of our whole life? If He died only for the sins which He knew we would commit before we were saved, but not for the sins after we are saved, then when must Jesus die again to make atonement for these sins, which He did not atone for on the Cross? You see, all our sins were borne by Him at Calvary, past, present, and future, before we were even born, and His resurrection is our proof and assurance of this fact, for we repeat, "the wages of sin is death," and one sin would have kept Christ in the tomb forever.

KEPT BY GRACE

Notice how this assurance of our security is stated by the Apostle Paul. In Romans 5:1, he says we are justified by faith. That takes care of the past and the present for us, but how about the future? Paul goes on:

> But God commendeth his love toward us, in that, while we were yet sinners, Christ died for us.
> Much more then, being now justified by his blood, we shall be saved from wrath through him.
> For if, when we were enemies, we were reconciled to God by the death of His Son, *much more*, being reconciled, we shall be saved [kept saved] by his life (Romans 5:8-10).

Justified by His death—Kept by His life.
Pardoned by His death—Declared righteous and just by His resurrection.

This should answer those who insist that after we are saved we can again be lost. But again we hear the old question repeated over and over and over again. Does this then mean that since we are saved by grace and cannot be lost again, we can now live as we please, and do as we want to? If we are free from the condemnation of the law, then can we become lawless? This question can be answered from the Word of God. The Bible is perfectly clear that we are saved by grace, and eternal life is *eternal,* but to say that it makes no difference how a Christian lives after he is saved, or what he does after he has been converted, is as far from the truth as anything can be. It does make a difference, and a tremendous difference. God does judge His people.

Before taking up this subject, may we point out again that there is a difference between *condemnation* and *judgment.* There is no condemnation for the believer, but there certainly is judgment. He will have to give an account for all his deeds, words, and even his thoughts, at the Judgment Seat of Christ. There is a payday coming for the Christian, as well as for the unsaved, and if you think that a Christian can live as he pleases, and get away with it, then listen carefully to the teaching of God's Word on this important subject.

Simply stated, the question is this: What happens to a believer, a Christian, who after he is saved goes back in sin and dies without full repentance? It is no use evading the issue. It is a valid, important question, and it must be given a plain and definite answer. What explanation do we have? The Bible clearly gives the answer, and it is the almost completely overlooked and neglected teaching of the Judgment Seat of Christ. Paul in speaking of believers says in II Corinthians 5:10,

> For we must all appear before the judgment seat of Christ; that every one may receive the things done in his body, according to that he hath done, whether it be good or bad.

Before taking up the study of this verse we must call your attention to one all-important fact. The Judgment Seat of Christ is not to be confused with the Great White Throne Judgment of Revelation 20. Unless we sharply distinguish between these two, the Judgment Seat of Christ and the Judgment of the Great White Throne, we shall never be able to understand either one. The Judgment Seat of Christ and the Great White Throne Judgment at the end of the world are separated in point of time by at least one thousand years. The Judgment Seat of Christ occurs before the Millennium. The Judgment of the Great White Throne occurs at the close of the Millennium, as clearly taught in Revelation 20, where we read that it will come after "the thousand years were finished."

At the Judgment Seat of Christ, before the Millennium, only believers will appear. Not a single unsaved person will be there. This is perfectly clear from every passage bearing on this important truth. It will include all the saved dead who will be resurrected at Jesus' coming, together with all the saved believers who will be living when Jesus comes to raise the believing dead. These will be caught up together to meet the Lord in the air, and then will follow the Judgment Seat of Christ.

In sharp contrast to this, only unbelievers, only the lost, will appear at the Judgment of the Great White Throne, one thousand years later. There will be no saved ones there at all. There will only be those who are lost and who have rejected the Lord Jesus Christ. The believers at the Judgment Seat of Christ before the thousand year reign will be judged on the basis of their works, and given their relative position in the Kingdom on the basis of this judgment. It has to do, therefore, with rewards only, and has nothing to do whatsoever with their salvation.

In the very same way, the wicked at the Judgment of the Great White Throne will also be judged according to their works (Revelation 20:12). This again has nothing to do with determining whether they are saved or lost. That was settled once for all when they died, and the door of opportunity was shut forever. This judgment on the basis of works is to determine their relative suffering in Hell (the degree of their punishment), based on the record of their works, their opportunities, and the light they have rejected. Both the judgment of the saved at the Judgment Seat of Christ before the Millennium, and the lost at the Great White Throne Judgment after the Millennium, will be on the basis of their works, and will determine the relative degree of rewards for the believers in the Kingdom, and the relative degree of suffering for the lost in Hell. Let me repeat, therefore, that neither has anything to do with deciding the eternal destiny of the saved or the lost. That was settled for the believer by his acceptance of Christ, and for the unbeliever by his rejection of the Lord Jesus Christ.

We have dwelt at some length on this because upon your proper comprehension of these basic truths depends your understanding of the chapters which are to follow on the judgments of the believer. Let me repeat, therefore, the Judgment Seat of Christ occurs *before* the Kingdom reign of Christ. The Great White Throne Judgment occurs *after* the Kingdom reign of Christ. The Judgment Seat of Christ is for believers only. The Great White Throne Judgment is for unbelievers and the lost only. The Judgment Seat of Christ is to judge the believer's works. The Great White Throne Judgment is to judge the unbeliever's works. At the Judgment Seat of Christ the believer will be assigned his proper place and reward in the Kingdom

on the basis of his record. At the Great White Throne Judgment
the unbeliever will be assigned to his proper place in Hell and
the degree of his punishment determined by the record of his life.

There are three judgments of the believer which are revealed
in the Word of God. They may be classified as *past, present* and
future. The first was completed on the Cross of Calvary when
Jesus said, "It is finished." That settled the *judgment for sin*
forever. To those who believe in the Lord Jesus Christ, God
immediately imputes a perfect righteousness, and they are saved
once and for all. The *sin* question is settled and the believers
have eternal life which can never be lost. In their position and
standing they are now complete in the Lord Jesus Christ, and
stand before God as though they had never sinned. The vilest,
lowest and filthiest sinner, as well as the most self-righteous one,
may therefore come to the Saviour and be instantly and eternally saved by faith, to receive a new life which can never die
because it is the life of God Himself. For all such, Hell is forever
past, and Heaven is their assured abode. Judgment (as far as
condemnation is concerned) is past forever, for it was all passed
upon the Lord Jesus Christ, and God now sees no sin *on* the
believer, because "He hath laid on him (Christ) the iniquity of
us all" (Isaiah 53:6).

> Verily, verily, I say unto you, He that heareth my word, and
> believeth on him that sent me, hath everlasting life, and shall
> not come into condemnation; but is passed from death unto
> life (John 5:24).

> There is therefore now no condemnation to them which
> are in Christ Jesus, who walk not after the flesh, but after
> the Spirit.
> For the law of the Spirit of life in Christ Jesus hath made
> me free from the law of sin and death (Romans 8:1, 2).

We would therefore emphasize again that salvation is all of
grace, and the moment that we accept Christ as Saviour the
judgment upon our sin is forever past. God imputes to us the
righteousness of His Son Jesus Christ and we are "accepted in
the beloved."

This judgment of our sins in the person of Jesus our substitute, is called *justification.* We have nothing in human experience with which to illustrate the act of justification. It has no
counterpart in human law. No court on earth, no judge among
men, no law which can be enacted, can declare a guilty man

justified. A governor can pardon, but he cannot justify or declare guiltless. No man can die for another's sin and remove the guilt from the criminal or justify him in any sense whatsoever. We just have nothing in human experience to even approach the meaning of justification. Only God can justify a sinner, declare a guilty man guiltless, pronounce an unjust man just; it defies human explanation.

Someone has said long ago that *justification* is an act of God whereby a guilty sinner is declared righteous and just in God's sight by the imputation of God's righteousness to him on the basis of the satisfactory and completed work of the Lord Jesus. This redemptive work of Christ consists of more than His atoning death on the cross. It includes His resurrection as well. The fact that Christ died for our sins according to the Scriptures cannot justify a single sinner. All the death of Christ could do was to pay the penalty of sin, but it does not make the sinner righteous. The death of Christ satisfies the demands of God's law; but if Jesus had done no more than die for our sins, we would be saved from Hell, without being able to enter Heaven. Justification, therefore, that act of God which declared us not only *pardoned* but also *justified* is accomplished through the resurrection of our Lord. The death of Christ paid the penalty of sin but it is through the resurrection that the sinner is declared righteous and not only pardoned. Thereafter he stands in the sight of God not as a pardoned sinner but as a justified saint, and is *in Christ*, before God, as though he had never in all his life committed one single sin. This justification is an act which is for all eternity. It cannot be repeated, but establishes the absolute security of the believer in Christ.

This of course raises the question, What happens if such an one, justified and saved, lives in or falls into sin? Suppose a believer who has been truly justified and born again, falls into sin and dies without confessing or repenting of that sin, how will God deal with such a person? Does grace cover it all, and will there be no judgment for such a believer? This is the thing we expect to take up in our next chapter.

Now before we close this chapter, one word to the unsaved. Your only hope is to acknowledge your sin, believe the promise of God, receive by faith the Lord Jesus Christ, and be saved for time and eternity. There is no other way. May God enable you to make the decision immediately. Amen.

Chapter Twenty-Four

WHOM THE LORD LOVETH

Is it true that the Bible teaching of grace and security leads to carelessness and license? What about Christians who have been truly born again, and then fall into sin? What about some who apparently were saved and then fall away and die without giving evidence of repentance? Is it true that when we are saved and all our sins of the past, present and future are put under the blood, it will then make no difference how we live? These questions of grave importance have been constantly asked, and we should be able to give intelligent answers. Various groups have sought to answer the question, What is God going to do with believers who fall into sin, and then die before they have an opportunity of repenting?

The Roman Catholic Church has its own answer in the doctrine of purgatory, which seeks to answer this puzzling question of unforgiven sin. The Arminians in general have their answer in the doctrine of falling from grace, or the teaching of losing salvation after we are saved. Then there are certain holiness groups who have still another answer. They say that the sanctified ones alone will be raptured at the Second Coming of the Lord Jesus Christ, and the others who have not been sanctified will have to pass through a part or all of the Tribulation period.

These are all sincere attempts, no doubt, to answer the question, What happens to believers who die in unconfessed sin? We believe that none of these answers is the correct one, however, in the light of the total teaching of Scripture. We therefore should ask ourselves, do we have a better answer? or do we have an answer at all? Before rejecting any of these others, we should be able to come up with a better one, and one which we believe is the Scriptural solution to this vexing problem.

We certainly cannot accept a doctrine which teaches that God will do nothing about unconfessed sin. Common sense alone, as well as the Bible, teaches that we cannot claim to be Christians and then continue in sin and have the Lord do nothing

161

about it. We should be able to give an intelligent answer to the question. Therefore, we would re-examine this problem in the light of Scripture, for we believe that the Bible definitely teaches that payday is coming, and that none is going to escape it. The one-sided teaching of grace, grace, grace, without the balancing truth of Christian responsibility as well, has given rise to a distorted and unscriptural view of salvation. There are many folks who talk of grace, saved by grace, kept by grace, but who leave the impression that "once saved, always saved" means that it makes no difference how the Christian lives and behaves after he is saved, and that everything is going to come out all right. They tell us that eternal life is *eternal*. Of course, there can be no argument here whatsoever that eternal life is *eternal*, but that very fact requires that we should live as is becoming of those who have received eternal life. The impression that if you are once saved, you can therefore live for the Devil, doing as you please and it will make no difference in the end, is the Devil's own lie. It is this thinking which is at the root of much of the worldliness and carnality of the church today with its resultant hatred, malice, misunderstanding, and splitting up of the body of believers. God is still a holy God, and there is a payday coming. God says that He will judge His people. Those who talk as though they can live as they please just because they are saved, are either not saved at all or else they sorely need the truth concerning the Judgment Seat of Christ and the fact that God does judge His people.

In our previous chapter on "Payday Is Coming," we pointed out the security of the believer by faith in the finished work of the Lord Jesus Christ. We then also introduced the truth that this is only one aspect of salvation, and that there are in actuality three judgments of the believer. The first is the judgment of the believer's sins, which was taken care of at Calvary, and is accomplished by our Lord Himself. This settles our salvation forever. But there is also a present judgment when God chastens His people and deals with them because of their walk and their conduct, and this has to do with their sanctification, and their enjoyment of salvation. Then there is a third judgment of the believer, which still is future; it is called in Scripture, the Judgment Seat of Christ, at which time all the works of the believer will be weighed, rewards will be given to those who have laid up spiritual treasures in Heaven, and there will be loss of rewards for those who have neglected the great gift of salvation and have come before the Judgment Seat unprepared. We are now ready to take up the second of these three judgments of the believer.

PRESENT JUDGMENT

Let me repeat again, that while the judgment for sin is past once and forever, and the judgment of our works is still in the future, the Lord does judge our walk daily, moment by moment. Now that we are saved, He wants us to walk as though we are truly redeemed people. For that reason He has made provision for our daily cleansing. Provision for this cleansing is in the Word of God, through the Holy Spirit, and is by the means of our intercessory High Priest at the right hand of God. He is there for the express purpose of receiving our confession daily as we come to Him.

> If we say that we have no sin, we deceive ourselves, and the truth is not in us.
> If we confess our sins, he is faithful and just to forgive us our sins, and to cleanse us from all unrighteousness.
> If we say that we have not sinned, we make him a liar, and his word is not in us (I John 1:8-10).

Our hope then lies not in denying our sinfulness as Christians, but rather in confessing our sins honestly before Him. When we do this, He is ever faithful and just to cleanse us from all unrighteousness. God wants His children clean, and He will have them clean. He will not for one moment. tolerate their continuing in sin. To refuse to confess and abandon our sins after we are saved calls for the intervention of the Lord in chastening, to the end that we may be cleansed. There are two ways of cleansing which the Lord utilizes. One is the gentle way, by the washing of the Word as we confess our sins and claim His forgiveness. If we refuse to do this and continue in unconfessed sin, then the Lord says, "I will have to take a hand in it myself, for I want you to be clean, though I may have to lay my hand upon you and lay you low, or even take you home to glory."

As an illustration of this great truth, Paul tells us in Ephesians 5:25,

> Husbands, love your wives, even as Christ also loved the church, and gave himself for it;

That he might sanctify and cleanse it with the washing of water by the word (Ephesians 5:25, 26).

Notice that the Lord says that He has loved the church and saved her, that He might *sanctify* and *cleanse* her. There is more to salvation than just escaping Hell or going to Heaven. God also wants us to be like the Lord Jesus Christ. The two words used in our Scripture, Ephesians 5:26, are "sanctify" and "cleanse," and these are by no means the same words in the Greek in their original meaning. The word "sanctify" refers to the cleansing of the believer by faith and by confession of sin. This is the gentle, easy, way available for all believers. But the word which is translated "cleanse" in this same verse is *katharesis* in the Greek. From this word comes our English word "cathartic." It really means a violent purging. When you as a Christian refuse to be sanctified by humble confession of sin, the Lord does not let you go on, and just forget it and overlook it, as some would have us believe. He may bear with us for a while, but sooner or later He is going to take a hand in the matter, for He will have His people clean. This chastening and cleansing may take various forms. Sometimes He may place you on a bed of sickness until you learn to confess your sin. Sometimes it may be by bereavement; sometimes by an affliction, and in extreme cases He may even take the believer home by death rather than permit him to go on living in unconfessed sin. A passage of Scripture which bears directly on this little-known but all-important truth is found in I Corinthians 11,

Wherefore whosoever shall eat this bread, and drink this cup of the Lord, unworthily, shall be guilty of the body and blood of the Lord.

But let a man examine himself, and so let him eat of that bread, and drink of that cup.

For he that eateth and drinketh unworthily, eateth and drinketh damnation to himself, not discerning the Lord's body.

For this cause many are weak and sickly among you, and many sleep.

For if we would judge ourselves, we should not be judged.

But when we are judged, we are chastened of the Lord, that we should not be condemned with the world (I Corinthians 11:27-32).

In this passage we must remember that God is speaking to believers, to men and women who have been born again and belong to the Lord Jesus Christ. And concerning these He says,

For this cause many are weak and sickly among you,
and many sleep (I Corinthians 11:30).

Paul is speaking about the consequence of unconfessed sin
in the life of the believer, and he says that because of this unconfessed sin many of the Corinthians were sick and weak, and
many of them were dead. Surely we must be impressed with the
fact that to be a Christian places upon us a great responsibility,
and we either allow the Word of God to cleanse us, or the Lord
will use more drastic means: sanctify and cleanse, or washing
and purging. The Christian may take his choice. He may either
be washed by the Word of God and by honest confession, or
allow God to administer His cathartic of chastening in the purging of evil out of his life.

Here, however, before going on, we would add a word of
explanation lest we should leave the impression that all sickness
and weakness and chastening of the Lord is because of unconfessed sin. This is not true by any means, as there are many other
reasons why God visits His people, in order to make them what
He wants them to be. We therefore would not make the statement that all sickness, weakness and death are because of sin
in the life of the believer; but, having said this, Paul does tell us
that in *many* cases this is the reason. To those believers who
harbor known sin in their lives, we must emphasize the warning
of the Apostle Paul by the love of Christ that the time will come
sooner or later when the Lord will lay His chastening hand
upon such, and place them across His disciplinary knee and put
them through the cleansing and purging of His chastening hand.
When the Lord gets through with this process, it may have been
a painful and very trying experience, but the result will be a
cleansing and a tenderness toward Him which had been lost
because of sin. Those of us who have gone through God's fire of
chastening know the painfulness of the experience, but also the
glory of the cleansing.

To the question, therefore, "Shall we sin that grace may
abound?" we have the answer of Paul,

. . . How shall we that are dead to sin, live any longer
therein? (Romans 6:2).

God will judge His people. There is a payday coming. Oh,
Christian, do not tempt the Lord to chasten you, but now bow
before Him, confess your sins, and be clean. Paul adds in this
one remarkable passage in Ephesians 5:27,

That he might present it [the Church] to himself a glorious church, not having spot, or wrinkle, or any such thing; but that it should be holy and without blemish.

Spots and *wrinkles*. Spots as we know are taken out by washing in water, but wrinkles are taken out only by a hot iron. Spots are made by contact with the world, and the Word will cleanse them. "If we confess our sins, he is faithful and just to forgive us," and He will wash out all the spots. However, wrinkles are caused by sitting in one position and refusing to move and exercise ourselves. It is the result of not being busy in the things of the Lord, and not occupying ourselves with those things which edify and sanctify. Continuance in this sort of a fruitless life will bring the chastening of the Lord, and we repeat again the warning of Paul:

For this cause many are weak and sickly among you, and many sleep (I Corinthians 11:30).

Yes, God will judge His people, and there is a payday coming.

However, before we close this message, we must have just one word with those of you who are unsaved. If the Lord will not allow sin in the life of the believer, but must deal with it in His grace for the purpose of cleansing, then what will He do to those who do not belong to Him, and who have rejected His Son the Lord Jesus Christ, and who continue in their unrepentant condition until it is too late? Well may the words of Peter in I Peter 4:17 be applied here:

For the time is come that judgment must begin at the house of God: and if it first begin at us, what shall the end be of them that obey not the gospel of God?

And if the righteous scarcely be saved, where shall the ungodly and the sinner appear? (I Peter 4:17, 18).

Remember, *payday is coming*!

Chapter Twenty-Five

FOR CONSCIENCE' SAKE

The Bible says:

> For whom the Lord loveth he chasteneth, and scourgeth every son whom he receiveth.
> If ye endure chastening, God dealeth with you as with sons; for what son is he whom the father chasteneth not?
> But if ye be without chastisement, whereof all are partakers, then are ye bastards, and not sons.
> Now no chastening for the present seemeth to be joyous, but grievous: nevertheless afterward it yieldeth the peaceable fruit of righteousness unto them which are exercised thereby (Hebrews 12:6-8, 11).

When the Lord saves a person, it is not merely to keep him from going to Hell, or to take him to Heaven when he dies, but His purpose is to make him ultimately like His Son, the Lord Jesus Christ Himself. From the moment a person is saved, God continues to deal with His children in this process of cleansing and conforming them to the image of His Son. This ultimate purpose of the Lord for every believer is going to be carried out, and if it is not accomplished in this life, it will be accomplished at the Judgment Seat of Christ.

In our previous message we saw in I Corinthians 11 that because of unwillingness on the part of the believer to submit to the warnings and chastenings of the Lord, God visited them with weakness and sickness and might even take the Christian Home prematurely, rather than have him continue in unconfessed sin. In I Corinthians 11 we read:

> But let a man examine himself, and so let him eat of that bread, and drink of that cup.
> For he that eateth and drinketh unworthily, eateth and drinketh damnation [judgment] to himself, not discerning the Lord's body.

167

For this cause many are weak and sickly among you, and many sleep.

For if we would judge ourselves, we should not be judged.

But when we are judged, we are chastened of the Lord, that we should not be condemned with the world (I Corinthians 11:28-32).

We remind you again that Paul is addressing these words to believers. The entire epistle of Paul to Corinth was written to those who had experienced salvation through faith in the Lord Jesus Christ. They were not saved because they were good, but because they had believed on the finished work of the Saviour. That they were Christians is assured by the very setting of the passage. Paul is speaking of the Lord's Table, and the sinner certainly has no place at the Table of the Lord. This is only for believers. Moreover, in verse 32 we read that they were chastened of the Lord that they might not be condemned with the world.

These Christians, Paul says, had among them many who were weak and sickly, and there were some who had died. The reason for their weakness, sickness and death was that they had refused to judge themselves. All sorts of evils were present in the Church at Corinth; dissensions, strife, sectarianism, divisions among the brethren, bitterness and malice, not to speak of the grosser sins of immorality and worldliness. These were all rampant in this carnal church. Instead of these Corinthians confessing their faults and judging sins in their lives, many had continued in them. Some had even come to the Table of the Lord drunken and brought reproach upon Christ before the whole world. Now the Table of the Lord is the special provision which the Lord has given to remind us that Christ died for our sins, and that He has made provision for our cleansing from sin; and if there is any place where sins ought to be judged, it is at the table of the Lord where Christians gather to be reminded of the awful price paid for their salvation, and to be reminded of their duty and responsibility to love one another as brethren. These Corinthian Christians, however, had come to the Table with unconfessed sin in their lives, yet judging one another instead of themselves. So Paul wants them to do two things: first, to *examine themselves*; and, second, *judge sin in their lives*. After that they should come to the breaking of the bread. Notice carefully, therefore, the words, "let a man examine *himself*." There are altogether too many Christians who feel that it is their duty and privilege to examine the other fellow. Because of some official position they may happen to hold, they are forever examining their brethren and judging other Christians, instead of examining themselves. The privilege of coming to the Lord's Table is an individual responsibility, between the believer and God who knows the heart—and He alone knows it. It is absolutely not the business of anyone else. When we examine our own hearts we will find enough there to judge and to keep us busy, yes, too busy, to ever try to examine someone else. Failure to follow this admonition to judge sin in our own lives results, according to Paul, in

PHYSICAL JUDGMENT

For he that eateth and drinketh unworthily, [that is, Christians who refuse to confess and judge their sins] eateth and drinketh damnation to himself, not discerning the Lord's body (I Corinthians 11:29).

Very unfortunately there is one word in this verse which is a mistranslation, and has given much misunderstanding. The word "damnation" should be translated "judgment" instead. The Greek word is *krineis* which means "judgment" and not "damnation." No Christian can be damned, nor condemned, but the Lord nevertheless does judge His people. Verse 32 of I Corinthians 11 says definitely that these should not be condemned with the world. The word "damnation" in verse 29 is the same root word translated "judge" in this same passage. This then is the teaching of the Apostle Paul, that the Christian who refuses to confess his sin, is going to be judged of the Lord.

WEAKNESS, SICKNESS, AND DEATH

This judging of the believer's unconfessed sin, says Paul, may take various forms. It is a physical judgment, and Paul names three things which may come upon the believer who continues in unconfessed sin. These three are called WEAKNESS, SICKNESS, and DEATH. Now right at this point let us remind you again, very emphatically, that not all weakness, sickness and death are the result of the chastening of the Lord. We go on to say that not even the greater part of the ailments of Christians are due to God's judgment upon unconfessed sin. There are occasions when God permits His children to suffer, as in the case of Paul and his thorn in the flesh, or in the tribulations of Job, when sinful actions are not the cause. If you are ill or suffering, and have honestly confessed before Him and accepted His forgiveness, then you may rest in the promise of God that "whom the Lord loveth he chasteneth." In such cases it is because of God's love, and not because He is judging sin in your life.

However, having said all this, we must still face the fact that Paul says, "many are weak and sickly among you, and many sleep," because of their unwillingness to yield in repentance to God.

We would address ourselves, therefore, to those of you who are believers in the Lord Jesus Christ. If you are harboring unconfessed sin in your life, you are really inviting the chastening judgment of the Lord. Countless Christians who are ill or weak, and probably facing death, could and might be well today, if they would only heed the warning of the Spirit of God, "let a man examine himself" (I Corinthians 11:28). God wants all His children clean, and He will not stop dealing with them until they are. This, of course, is not true of the unconverted at all. God does not chasten them. He leaves them alone, and permits them to go on in their sin, because their judgment will come in their eternal condemnation. God does not spank the Devil's children, but only His own. He will condemn the unbelievers later on. If, however, you are a child of God, then you are subject to His chastening now. How applicable, therefore, the passage in Hebrews with which we began this chapter:

> . . . My son, despise not thou the chastening of the Lord, nor faint when thou art rebuked of him:
> For whom the Lord loveth he chasteneth, and scourgeth every son whom he receiveth.
> If ye endure chastening, God dealeth with you as with sons; for what son is he whom the father chasteneth not?
> But if ye be without chastisement, whereof all are partakers, then are ye bastards, and not sons.
> Now no chastening for the present seemeth to be joyous, but grievous: nevertheless afterward it yieldeth the peaceable fruit of righteousness unto them which are exercised thereby (Hebrews 12:5-8, 11).

From this passage we notice two outstanding things: first, the Lord chastens His own because He wants them clean and because He loves them; and then secondly, this chastening results in peace only to those who are exercised thereby. We therefore ask, what about those Christians who are not exercised by the chastening, but instead they murmur and rebel? Paul says, "afterward it yieldeth the peaceable fruit of righteousness unto them which are exercised thereby." God has a way of dealing also with those who are not exercised by their chastening and do not repent and turn from their evil ways. God must then do a further work on them, and if His chastening here and now does not bear the desired fruit, they will be dealt with at the Judgment Seat of Christ, which we take up in a later chapter. This will occur when the Lord comes to judge His saints.

Untimely Death

While we believe that there is a time appointed for every man to die, including the believer, it is also true that the Christian may in a certain sense die an untimely death. This fact Paul states clearly when he says that because of the unwillingness to confess their sins, many have fallen asleep. The Lord loves His children so much that He simply will not permit them to continue in sin, but sooner or later will send upon them sickness and weakness; and if they still continue to rebel, He may even take them Home to glory. The Lord would rather take you unto Himself and let you settle it at the Judgment Seat of Christ, than to have you continue further in your defilement and rebellion. Now I realize that this is an unpleasant truth, and yet we believe that it is one which, if given heed to, will result in a peace and a return of blessing and assurance that many have lost.

Are you today experiencing the chastening hand of the Lord? If so, have you asked yourself why it is that you are passing through these trials and tribulations. First of all, it is because He loves you so. It is certainly not because God is angry, but entirely because His love will not allow you to go on in defilement, for He wants you to be like the Lord Jesus Christ. If you, therefore, will submit yourself humbly underneath the chastening hand of God and be exercised by it, and learn the lesson which God would have you learn during the time that you are laid aside, it will result in the peaceable fruit of righteousness in your life.

Not now but in the coming years;
It may be in the better land
We'll read the meaning of our tears,
And then, some day, we'll understand.
Maxwell Cornelius

It is enough for now to know that all of His dealings with us are in love, and for our profit, no matter how painful they may be at times. And so I would like to ask the question, Is God dealing with you personally? If so, examine your heart, and see just what God is trying to accomplish in your life. It may be that there is still something there which must be corrected, and He is trying to cleanse it by this particular message. Maybe your sickness is one which will not respond to medicine or surgery because God is seeking to cleanse you from something you have never really surrendered unto Him. While we thank God for all the means and methods He has given to us for the relief and cure of our physical ailments, we must also recognize that all the doctors and nurses and medicine in the world are unable to relieve some conditions which may be the result of a stubborn resistance to the will of God and an unwillingness to confess our sins. We believe that the epistle of James gives us definite teaching along this line:

Is any among you afflicted? let him pray. Is any merry? let him sing psalms.

Is any sick among you? let him call for the elders of the church: and let them pray over him, anointing him with oil in the name of the Lord:

And the prayer of faith shall save the sick, and the Lord shall raise him up; and if he have committed sins, they shall be forgiven him.

Confess your faults one to another, and pray one for another, that ye may be healed (James 5:13-16).

We believe that two mistakes have been made in trying to interpret this passage. First of all, there are those who reject this entirely, saying that it does not apply to this dispensation, and telling us James wrote to the Jews, and therefore this has no application for us at all. That, of course, we believe is wrong, for James says, "let him call for the elders of the *church.*" The second error is perpetuated by those who go to another extreme. They claim that this passage supports the modern methods of divine healing for all who are sick. They quote it to fortify their racketeering campaign for healing, while they prey upon the weakness and gullibility of the sick and incapacitated. Notice, the healer goes to the sick one here in James' epistle, while the modern, divine healer (so-called) today, requires the sick ones to come to their fantastical and fanatical meetings. Moreover, it is the prayer of the elders that does the work, and not the faith of the sick one. Yet today, when their methods fail, they invariably excuse themselves by saying, "Well, she (or he) did not have faith enough to be healed." Such ignorance is appalling if it is honest, and disgusting if it is not.

LIMITED APPLICATION

James is speaking of certain cases of sickness only, which were undoubtedly due to unconfessed sin. This is evident from the passage. Will you read it again? He says,

> . . . the prayer of faith shall save the sick . . .

It does not say, as it is usually quoted, the prayer of faith shall *heal* the sick, but it says definitely, "shall save the sick." The healing depends upon something else. It must be preceded by confession, and so James says,

> And the prayer of faith shall save the sick, and the Lord shall raise him up; and if he have *committed sins*, they shall be forgiven him (James 5:15).

Now notice the very next word in the following verse: *confess—*

> *Confess* your faults one to another, and pray one for another, that ye may be healed (James 5:16).

First, confession and prayer, and then healing. To apply this passage, therefore, to all cases of sickness is both foolish and unscriptural. When you are sick you need a doctor. That is what our Lord Himself says when He states in Luke 5:31,

> . . . They that are whole need not a physician; but they that are sick (Luke 5:31).

Surely words cannot be plainer than those from the lips of Jesus. So when you get sick, call a good, reliable physician, and then believe that God uses means for the restoration of health. But always observe two rules: first of all, be sure there is nothing in your life that needs to be corrected and confessed before Him; and then secondly, submit the result entirely to His care. Do not demand of the Lord that you should be healed, but always make your prayer, "Not my will, but Thine be done." It is more important to be submissive to the will of God, than to experience physical healing. If it is God's will that you can serve Him better in your present condition, than in the condition in which you would like to be, then God's will is always best. We should learn in all of our petitions to Him, to practice the spirit of the prayer of our Saviour Himself, "Not my will, but Thine be done."

This chapter, of course, has been for believers, but when we realize the holiness of God and how He will not tolerate sin unjudged even in the life of the believer, what a terrible thing it must be to fall into the hands of a living God without the blood of the Lord Jesus Christ, and without a covering for sins. We therefore repeat again the words in I Peter 4:17,

> For the time is come that judgment must begin at the house of God: and if it first begin at us, what shall the end be of them that obey not the gospel of God?
> And if the righteous scarcely be saved, where shall the ungodly and the sinner appear? (I Peter 4:17, 18).

Chapter Twenty-Six

THE FINAL RECKONING

The believer in Christ is free from the law (Romans 8:2), delivered from the law (Romans 7:6), and dead to the law (Galatians 2:19); for Christ is the end of the law to every one that believeth (Romans 10:4). This does not mean, however, that the believer is not responsible to God and will not be judged by Him for his conduct after he is saved. God will certainly require an accounting of how this freedom and liberty has been used or abused. There is a payday coming for the believer. In an earlier chapter we saw the responsibility of the believer in this present walk, and the provision God has made for his cleansing and forgiveness. We turn now to the judgment of the believer's works at the Judgment Seat of Christ. For our Scripture will you turn to I Corinthians 3:11-15, and let me remind you that this is written to believers only. It has nothing to do with salvation, but is a matter of rewards for service and loss of rewards for unfaithfulness.

> For other foundation can no man lay than that is laid, which is Jesus Christ.
> Now if any man build upon this foundation gold, silver, precious stones, wood, hay, stubble;
> Every man's work shall be made manifest: for the day shall declare it, because it shall be revealed by fire; and the fire shall try every man's work of what sort it is.
> If any man's work abide which he hath built thereupon, he shall receive a reward (I Corinthians 3:11-14).

Then notice especially the 15th verse:

> If any man's work shall be burned, he shall suffer loss: but he himself shall be saved; yet so as by fire (I Corinthians 3:15).

This was the thing that Paul feared above all things. He did not fear losing his salvation. He was perfectly assured of that, but he feared losing out on the reward and the crown at the end of the road. He feared that after a lifetime of preaching he might in a careless moment succumb to the flesh and be set aside and taken out of service. That he did not fear losing his salvation is clear from his own words. He says in II Timothy 1:12,

> . . . I know whom I have believed, and am persuaded that he is able to keep that which I have committed unto him against that day (II Timothy 1:12).

This is perfectly clear then, that Paul was not worried about his ultimate salvation, but there was something Paul did greatly fear. He says in I Corinthians 9, verse 24,

> Know ye not that they which run in a race run all, but one receiveth the prize? So run, that ye may obtain.
> I therefore so run, not as uncertainly; so fight I, not as one that beateth the air:
> But I keep under my body, and bring it into subjection: lest that by any means, when I have preached to others, I myself should be a castaway (I Corinthians 9:24, 26, 27).

How this passage has confused people; but notice carefully, Paul is not talking about salvation but about rewards and the crown for faithfulness. He is talking about running a race. Surely a sinner must not run to get into Heaven or to obtain salvation. This is a free gift. A dead sinner cannot run. Paul knew that salvation does not depend upon our running or upon our works, but upon the grace of God. What Paul feared most was that after a life of service he might play the fool and lose out on the reward and make it necessary for him to be put on the shelf. It is possible for a Christian to fall away, until God retires him from service; and he will then be dealt with at the Judgment Seat of Christ, to see all the wood, the hay, and the stubble go up in smoke, and he be saved so as by fire. The word "castaway" is translated in the American Standard Version (1901) as "rejected." It means to be disqualified for a reward. And so we repeat again, it has nothing to do with the matter of salvation.

WHEN WILL THIS OCCUR?

Before going on further with this subject, we must first of all determine at what time and what place the Judgment Seat of

Christ is to occur. There are many Scripture passages dealing with this truth, but they have been sadly neglected, and the average believer knows little or nothing concerning it. The preaching of a gospel which teaches that the saint may live as he pleases and no ill results to follow, is so pleasing to the flesh, that the teaching of the Judgment Seat of Christ has been passed by lightly and has been virtually neglected. Note carefully, therefore, a number of passages which deal with this matter.

> Therefore judge nothing before the time, until the Lord come, who both will bring to light the hidden things of darkness, and will make manifest the counsels of the hearts: and then shall every man have praise of God (I Corinthians 4:5).

> But why dost thou judge thy brother? or why dost thou set at nought thy brother? for we shall all stand before the judgment seat of Christ (Romans 14:10).

> And, behold, I come quickly; and my reward is with me, to give every man according as his work shall be (Revelation 22:12).

> And now, little children, abide in him; that, when he shall appear, we may have confidence, and not be ashamed before him at his coming (I John 2:28).

> Wherefore we labour, that, whether present or absent, we may be accepted of him.
> For we must all appear before the judgment seat of Christ; that every one may receive the things done in his body, according to that he hath done, whether it be good or bad (II Corinthians 5:9, 10).

These and many other passages clearly indicate that the time of the Judgment Seat of Christ will be when the Lord comes for His saints. When this has happened there will follow a time of terrible judgment on this earth during the Tribulation period, when the Lord will judge the nations of the earth and the nation of Israel. It will be a time of judgment not only on the earth, but in the air as well, for then it will be that the Lord will judge His people. During this time, between the Rapture of the Church and the Second Coming of the Lord, there will be a time of preparation for the Bride in anticipation of the Wedding of the Lamb, and the return of the Bride with her Lord to the earth. Before this happens, the Bride must be clean. When the Lord calls the Church out of the world before the Tribulation, many members of His Bride will not yet be ready. Their garments will be soiled and defiled and they will be caught unawares, and before the Lord does anything else, therefore, the Bride must be made ready. This is the function of the Judgment Seat of Christ. It is to this time that Paul refers when he warns the believer to be careful what manner of material he builds on the true foundation.

Two Classes of Christians

At this coming of the Lord there will be two kinds of believers: spiritual and carnal. Both will be saved, but what a difference in their works and their rewards! While the faithful ones shall receive rewards at the hands of the Saviour, the others who have lived carelessly and have not been their best for Christ shall pass through the fires of the Judgment Seat, until all of the wood, hay and stubble has been burned away, and the dross has been consumed. Then the little of gold, silver and precious stones which they may have accumulated will be purified and separated from their combustible works. This will not by any means be a happy experience. There will undoubtedly be much of regret and sorrow, and Paul says that they shall *suffer* loss: but they themselves shall be saved; yet so as by fire. There will undoubtedly be a great deal of confessing up there which should have been done down here. Many, many tears will be shed over opportunities wasted and rewards that have been lost. It is not in vain that the words, "And God shall wipe away all tears from their eyes," are not spoken until *after* the Judgment Seat of Christ and His glorious reign begins.

Rewards and Promotions

These two classes of Christians (spiritual and carnal) who will be caught up at the Rapture are described by many figures in the Bible. We have seen them in I Corinthians 3 as those who will "receive a reward," and those who shall "suffer loss." John says in the passage quoted earlier that some will have *confidence* while others will be *ashamed* at His appearing. Some will have "an abundant entrance," while others will be "saved, yet so as by fire." In II Timothy 2 we are told:

If we suffer, we shall also reign with him: if we deny him, he also will deny us (II Timothy 2:12).

The position of the believer in the Kingdom reign *after* the Lord comes, will therefore be determined on the basis of how much "gold, silver and precious stones" will be left after the fires of the Judgment Seat of Christ have burned away the wood, hay and stubble. When this period of judgment is drawing to a close and the Lord is preparing to return with His Bride to take the Kingdom, every single saint will be clean, but all will not have the same reward. Some will hold an exalted position in the Kingdom, and others will have a place of lesser authority and service. All of this will be determined on the basis of what we have done for Christ during the brief period of our Christian life. How tremendously important becomes each day of opportunity and every privilege for service which we have here below! The opportunities for serving Him today which we have neglected, will take just that much from the rewards we will receive up there.

The Bride Is Ready!

Finally at the close of the Judgment Seat of Christ, the Bride has been made ready! She is now arrayed in two robes of righteousness. One is the *robe of salvation* which was received the moment the sinner took Christ as Saviour. The other robe is the *robe of rewards*, and is briefly but dramatically described in Revelation 19, just before the glorious return of the Lord Jesus to reign:

Let us be glad and rejoice, and give honour to him: for the marriage of the Lamb is come, and his wife hath made herself ready.

And to her was granted that she should be arrayed in fine linen, clean and white: for the fine linen is the righteousness of saints (Revelation 19:7, 8).

Notice carefully the words, *his wife hath made herself ready.* Evidently she was not ready before. Now this passage in Revelation 19 is seven years after the Rapture in the fourth chapter of Revelation. In Revelation 4:1, 2, the Church is caught away from the earth and never appears again in the book of Revelation until she is seen here just before the glorious return of the Lord. In chapters 6 to 19 of Revelation, God's judgments are described as being poured out upon the earth, while at the same time God is also judging the Bride in the air in preparation for the reign. Now, after the cleansing is complete, she reappears *clean and white*. The clean white robe, we are told is *her righteousness*. The original word translated "righteousness of saints" is really "the righteous acts of the saints." Her robe consists of the material she herself has provided here upon the earth; and now, cleansed from all wood, hay, and stubble, she is to be arrayed for the wedding in the robe of her own making.

What kind of a robe will you wear, my friend? Is your life a life of service and righteousness, or a life of selfishness and fleshliness? Are you seeking your own, or are you seeking the glory of God? What a disappointment it will be to stand before Him, and to find that we have forfeited and bartered away the opportunity for a place of highest honor in His Kingdom, for a few of the fleeting, evanescent, paltry pleasures of this temporary life. I do not know whether we will sing the songs up there which we sing down here, but if we do, I imagine many members of the Bride will have to sing the song with sorrow and tears,

> Oh, the years of sinning wasted;
> Could I but recall them now.
> I would bring them to my Master;
> At His feet I'd humbly bow.

SHALL WE SIN?

We believe that this truth of the Judgment Seat of Christ is a needed truth for these days in which we live. There has been a great deal of unbalanced preaching of grace, as though the very fact that we are not under law, but entirely under grace, gives the Christian the right to live as he pleases. However, the Bible says that there is a payday coming. As a result the Church of Jesus Christ has lost her testimony and become a reproach before the world with her bickering, malice, and selfishness.

Before we close this message, there is one lesson I want to drive home, and it is this. We are truly saved by grace, and grace alone, without the works of the law. Every believer, however, will have to give an account of what he has done with this grace, of every deed and word which he has committed and spoken, from the day he was saved until the final day of his life here on earth ends. We shall be called upon to give an account of what we have done with our time, our opportunities, and our talents. The Apostle Paul says, "work out your own salvation with fear and trembling" (Philippians 2:12). This is the responsibility of the believer. We have received salvation as the free gift of God, and now it is our responsibility as to what we do with that which we have received. Every man will be called to render an account of stewardship, those who have received one talent as well as those who have received ten; the servant whose pound gained ten pounds, as well as the one who hid his pound and came back before the Lord with nothing at all.

There is a little story which has often been told, but can bear frequent repeating. It is only a story, but it illustrates a great truth.

According to the narrative, a wealthy Christian woman had a poor gardener who worked for her for many years. She was selfish and worldly, while the gardener was faithful in his service. He lost no opportunity to witness for the Lord Jesus Christ, while the wealthy matron was riding in her luxurious limousine enjoying the selfish pleasures of her wealth and of her position. Then both the rich lady and her gardener died.

The poor man went home to glory just a little while before his employer. When she was ushered into Heaven and greeted, an angel came to her and said, "Now I will show you the home which has been prepared for you here. You are a child of God and of course you have a mansion in the sky." So they walked along a beautiful avenue with resplendent buildings, and when she saw a particularly beautiful one she murmured to herself, "That must be mine. I remember how I gave a thousand dollars to missions and another thousand to charity. Surely this must be my home." But the angel answered, "No, that belongs to your wash woman."

The next beautiful building, to her surprise, belonged to her gardener, and she became all thrilled at the thought of what a magnificent home she would receive, if these poor, humble ones who had been able to do so little for the Lord were entitled to such magnificent mansions and dwelling places.

Then they came to the end of the street and there stood a very small, unimpressive little cottage, scantily furnished and unattractive, and over the door was written her name. She couldn't believe her eyes, and shuddered and cried out, "There must be some mistake. Surely this is not mine. How is it that I who have given so much in life should have so little compared with those who have done but a fraction of what I have done?"

The angel answered, "It is not *what*, or *how much* you have done, but what you might have done and did not do which determines your home up here. We build here only with the material which is sent up from earth. That which is sent in the energy of the flesh and in selfishness is rejected before it goes into the new home. The poor gardener did all that he could; hence, his great castle. And you while you did far more in the mass than he did, did only a fraction of what you could and might have done." The rewards are going to be on the percentage basis.

This is the principle of the Judgment Seat of Christ. It is not a matter of how much we have done for the Lord, but how much we could have done and left undone. Someone has aptly said, God never looks at the amount on the face of our check, but He looks at the balance on the stub. It is not how much we have given but how much we have held back for ourselves. The greater our talents, the greater our responsibility; the greater our opportunities, the greater our debt to the Lord will be. We can do no better than to close with the words of our Lord Jesus Christ Himself in Luke 12:

> And that servant, which knew his lord's will, and prepared not himself, neither did according to his will, shall be beaten with many stripes.
>
> But he that knew not, and did commit things worthy of stripes, shall be beaten with few stripes. For unto whomsoever much is given, of him shall be much required: and to whom men have committed much, of him they will ask the more (Luke 12:47, 48).